Women in the Arts

Agnes de Mille

He who neglects the arts when he is young
has lost the past and is dead to the future.

—Sophocles, *Fragments*

WOMEN in the ARTS

Agnes de Mille

Judy L. Hasday, Ed.M.

Introduction by
Congresswoman Betty McCollum
Minnesota, Fourth District
Member, National Council on the Arts

CHELSEA HOUSE
PUBLISHERS
A Haights Cross Communications Company

Philadelphia

To Elyse Nicole Cohen, the Girldancer who dances her own path—
Always Believe, Dream, Embrace life.
And remember, I love you—
Aunt Judy

CHELSEA HOUSE PUBLISHERS
VP, NEW PRODUCT DEVELOPMENT Sally Cheney
DIRECTOR OF PRODUCTION Kim Shinners
CREATIVE MANAGER Takeshi Takahashi
MANUFACTURING MANAGER Diann Grasse

Staff for AGNES DE MILLE
EDITOR Patrick M.N. Stone
PRODUCTION EDITOR Megan Emery
PHOTO EDITOR Sarah Bloom
SERIES & COVER DESIGNER Terry Mallon
LAYOUT 21st Century Publishing and Communications, Inc.

A Haights Cross Communications ⌐ Company

www.chelseahouse.com

First Printing

1 3 5 7 9 8 6 4 2

Library of Congress Cataloging-in-Publication Data

Hasday, Judy L., 1957–
    Agnes de Mille/by Judy Hasday.
      p. cm.—(Women in the arts)
Includes index.
Contents: Rodeo comes to broadway—A prominent family tree—
Transformed by a ballerina—The long search for success begins—No
one dances in America—Crisscrossing the Atlantic—Breakthrough
with an American ballet—A life and career complete.
    ISBN 0-7910-7457-9   0-7910-7951-1 PB
    1. De Mille, Agnes. 2. Dancers—United States—Biography—Juvenile
literature. 3. Choreographers—United States—Biography—Juvenile
literature. [1. De Mille, Agnes. 2. Dancers. 3. Choreographers. 4. Women—
Biography.] I. Title. II. Series.
GV1785.D36H37 2003
792.8'092—dc21
                                                        2003014168

Table of Contents

Introduction

Congresswoman Betty McCollum

Minnesota, Fourth District
Member, National Council on the Arts

I am honored to introduce WOMEN IN THE ARTS, a continuing series of books about courageous, talented women whose work has changed the way we think about art and society. The women highlighted in this series were persistent, successful, and at times controversial. They were unafraid to ask questions or challenge social norms while pursuing their work. They overcame barriers that included discrimination, prejudice, and poverty. The energy, creativity, and perseverance of these strong women changed our world forever.

Art plays a critical role in all our lives, in every culture, and especially in the education of young people. Art can be serious, beautiful, functional, provocative, spiritual, informative, and illuminating. For all of the women in this series, their respective forms of artistic expression were a creative exploration and their professional calling. Their lives and their work transformed the world's perception of a woman's role in society.

In reading this series, I was struck by common themes evident in these women's lives that can provide valuable lessons for today's young women.

One volume tells the story of Coco Chanel, the first fashion designer to create clothing for women that was both attractive and utile. Chanel was one of the first women to run a large, successful business in the fashion industry. Today, it is hard to imagine the controversy Chanel stirred up simply by making women's clothing beautiful, comfortable, and practical. Chanel understood that women wanted a sense of style and professionalism in their fashion, as men had in theirs.

Chanel's extraordinary success demonstrates that we should not be afraid to be controversial. Even today, women of all ages worry far too much about stepping on toes or questioning authority. To make change, in our own lives or in our community, we need to stand up and speak out for our beliefs. The women of this series often defied convention and ruffled some feathers, but they never stopped. Nina Simone sang beautifully, but she also spoke out against the injustice of racism, regardless of how it affected her career.

It is equally important for us women to ask ourselves, "What do I want from my life?" We all struggle to answer this deceptively simple question. It takes courage to answer it honestly, but it takes far more courage to answer the question and then *act* on that answer. For example, Agnes de Mille realized she had "nothing to lose by being direct." She stuck to her vision for *Rodeo,* insisted on the set and composer she envisioned, and eventually produced her ballet—the way she wanted to. She believed in her vision, and the result was a great success. Dorothea Lange, having decided she wanted to become a photographer, asked for photography jobs, even though she had no experience and it was a profession that few women pursued.

In our society, we expect that all people should be treated with respect and dignity, but this has not always been true. Nina Simone faced discrimination and overcame social norms that promoted racial injustice. She confronted prejudice and disrespect directly, sometimes refusing to perform when an audience was unruly or rude. One evening, when she was only eleven years old, she even delayed her performance until her own parents were allowed to sit in the front row—seats that they had been asked to vacate for white people. Her demand for respect took courage.

Women's equality not only benefits women, but also brings a unique perspective to the world. For example, the brilliance of Dorothea Lange's photography was in large part due to her empathy for her subjects. She knew that to tell their story, she needed to earn their trust and to truly understand their lives.

Each of these women used her art to promote social justice. Coco Chanel used her designs to make women's lives easier and more comfortable, while Nina Simone was as committed to civil rights as she was to her music. Dorothea Lange's photographs convinced Washington of the need to establish sanitary camps for migrant families, and Virginia Woolf's writing pushed the question of equal rights for women.

Because the women in these books, and so many others like them, took risks and challenged society, women today have more opportunity than ever before. We have access to equal education, and we are making great strides in the workplace and in government.

As only the second woman from Minnesota ever elected to serve in Congress, I know how important it is to have strong female role models. My grandmothers were born in a time when women did not have the right to vote, but their granddaughter is now a Member of Congress. Their strength, wisdom, and courage inspire me. Other great women, such as Congresswoman Barbara Jordan and Congresswoman Shirley Chisholm, also inspired me with their leadership and determination to overcome gender and racial discrimination to serve in Congress with distinction.

Dorothea Lange once said, "I have learned from everything, and I'm constantly learning." I know that I too am constantly learning. I hope the women in this series will inspire you to learn and to lead with courage and determination. Art, as a profession or a hobby, can be either an expression or an agent of change. We need to continue to encourage women to add their voices to our society through art.

The women profiled in this series broke barriers, followed their hearts, refused to be intimidated, and changed our world. Their lives and successes should be a lesson to women everywhere. In addition, and importantly, they created lasting and meaningful art. I hope that you will enjoy this series as much as I have.

Rodeo Comes to Broadway

The choreographic process is exhausting. It happens on one's feet after hours of work, and the energy required is roughly the equivalent of writing a novel and winning a tennis match simultaneously.
—Agnes de Mille, *Dance to the Piper*

For fourteen years Agnes de Mille had worked toward this moment—and those were only the years she had worked professionally. From the moment she'd watched Russian prima ballerina Anna Pavlova leap into the air, then land posed onstage, her "strong forthright taut plunging leg balanced on the poised arc of the foot, the other leg stretched to the horizon like the wing of a bird" (*Piper*, 40), de Mille's life course was determined. Now in her late thirties and still in search of the breakthrough choreographic production of her career, de Mille stood offstage dressed in her *Rodeo* costume—cowboy

De Mille as the Cowgirl, *Rodeo*, 1951. Whenever possible, Agnes de Mille danced the lead role of her shows on opening night. It is especially fitting that *Rodeo* should become the breakthrough production of de Mille's career, for the role of the Cowgirl mirrors her own life story. The production showcased a style of dance and choreography that pioneered an era of Broadway history.

boots, slacks, a Texas hat—with a bow attached to the single braid in her hair.

The seats of the Metropolitan Opera House were filled with an eagerly waiting audience. As de Mille listened to the orchestra overture, she hoped this work would finally place her among the other great modern dance pioneers, such as Isadora Duncan and her friend and colleague Martha Graham. American audiences were not familiar with the kind of choreography created by de Mille, in which elements of modern dance and ballet were blended in dance numbers that were woven into the plotline of a theatrical play. Would the audience appreciate dancers lurching across the stage on imaginary horses, or a solo ballet depicting rejection and despair performed by a dancer dressed as a cowgirl?

De Mille's idea for *Rodeo* had actually been born several years earlier, when she attended a Saturday night dance while teaching at the Perry-Mansfield Camp (a performing arts camp for girls) in Steamboat Springs, Colorado, during the summer of 1935. When the musicians began playing "Turkey in the Straw," de Mille improvised, creating her own version of a hoedown. She had seen square dancing before, but had never participated. Dancing solo to the beat of the music, she found it awe-inspiring. De Mille biographer Carol Easton explains de Mille's enthusiasm:

> She thought the old-fashioned courtesies romantic, the ranch hands the epitome of masculinity, and the designs of the dances intriguing. She had idealized cowboys since her childhood, when the extras who worked in her uncle's movies would ride into Cecil's yard, swoop her and her cousins up, and gallop around the block with the children clinging to the horns of their saddles. (Easton, 149)

De Mille's enthusiasm for a Western-style ballet might have gone no further if she hadn't been in the right place at the right time. Tired of always relying on her mother's financial assistance, and with no real prospects for dance work, de Mille had decided to get a job learning merchandising at a department store. Still wanting to keep up with her dancing, though, de Mille continued to take ballet classes. On her way to a class one day, she bumped into the wife of the scenographer and author Irving Deakin; she mentioned to de Mille that the Ballet Russe de Monte Carlo was going to put on a new work. Deakin was suggesting to the Ballet's director, Sergei Denham, that he commission de Mille for the work, and he wanted to know whether she had a scenario she could present. Even though she didn't, de Mille assured Deakin's wife that she did. She raced back to her small New York apartment to get to work.

In her book *Dance to the Piper*, de Mille describes the process:

> I went home and locked myself in for three days. I'd better use dance steps I was sure of. It would be horrible to get stuck with all those fancy Russians standing around so I decided to enlarge on the *Rodeo* studies and use sections of choreography already worked out. Draining great pots of tea, I wrote it all out, and then it seemed simply awful. But in a spirit of total despair I submitted it anyway and was summoned to my first interview with the boss of the Ballet Russe de Monte Carlo, Sergei Ivanovitch Denham. (De Mille, 204–205)

De Mille envisioned *Rodeo* in four scenes. The adolescent love story takes place on a ranch in Colorado. In the first scene, the wranglers are readying to participate in a rodeo. A young cowgirl appears in pants and imitates the cowboys' mannerisms and behavior. Once the rodeo begins, the cowboys show off their riding and roping skills to a small group of girls from town who have come to watch the men in action. The Cowgirl, who has a huge crush on the Head Wrangler, tries to grab his attention by competing alongside the other wranglers. She only makes a fool of herself, and the Wrangler expels the Cowgirl from the corral. He then leaves, escorting the rancher's beautiful daughter. Everyone else follows, leaving the Cowgirl alone. She dances a heartrending solo before collapsing to the ground in tears as the scene concludes.

The second scene opens with loud clapping and stamping boots as the lights go up, revealing a group of men and women engaging in a lively square dance. The dancers and caller accelerate the steps, going faster and faster until the dance reaches its whirling conclusion.

In the next scene, couples dance at a party in the rancher's house. The Cowgirl, still dressed like a wrangler, watches from outside. The Champion Roper comes along, befriends the Cowgirl, and teaches her how to dance. She is actually enjoying herself until she sees the Wrangler pairing off with the rancher's daughter. The scene ends with the Cowgirl falling to the ground once again, sobbing.

In the final scene, the men and women are choosing partners for a square dance. No one picks the Cowgirl, and she runs offstage, humiliated. The hoedown begins, with each couple trying to outdo the others. The Cowgirl reappears dressed traditionally as a girl, in a red dress and with a ribbon in her hair. She is partnered with each of the men one by one and outdances them all. Then the Wrangler steps in, and he manages to tire her out. She collapses in his arms, and they "live happily ever after." (In the final version of the ballet, the Roper challenges the Wrangler, then kisses the Cowgirl, who realizes that she actually loves *him*.)

When de Mille met with Denham, she found him to be soft-spoken and dedicated to the art and beauty of ballet. Still, his dominion over his dance company was obvious. During rehearsals, he sat at center stage in a chair with his name painted on it, so he was right in the middle of the rehearsal. No one had ever questioned Denham's presence in the wings, at the back of the theater watching with guests, or even just walking in during a rehearsal—that is, not until he met Agnes de Mille.

De Mille had always been rather strong-willed in every aspect of her life except the personal—with her mother and father and the various men with whom she had been romantically involved. De Mille figured she had nothing to lose by being direct, as this was going to be her last job before joining the department store. She told Denham that she wanted the composer Aaron Copland to write the musical score. Denham wanted a big red barn as part of the scenery; de Mille rejected the idea. Denham wanted only one backdrop; de Mille and her scenographer, Oliver Smith, insisted on the two sketches they presented to him. She was to dance the opening night of every season and to have complete artistic control. Eventually, and without much resistance, Denham agreed to all of de Mille's terms. He purchased *Rodeo* for $500.

Copland agreed to write the score for the show. He had already composed scores for ballet, including Lincoln Kirstein's *Billy the Kid*. De Mille sat with Copland and blocked out the score almost minute by minute. When she heard the entire musical score, it was actually played by Copland and a then-unknown young musician named Leonard Bernstein. De Mille was ecstatic with the result. In the meantime, Oliver Smith began transferring his backdrop sketches to actual scenery paintings. It was time to begin rehearsing with the dancers, so de Mille boarded a train for California, where the Ballet Russe de Monte Carlo troupe was on tour. While in Los Angeles, she stayed at her father's house.

De Mille held the first rehearsal for *Rodeo* with the male dancers at what had been the studio of Carmelita Maracci, a passionate Italian dancer whom de Mille had met years before in Los Angeles. Standing before her were nineteen intimidatingly muscled males with sculpted bodies who were classically trained ballet dancers. De Mille had never worked with more than one man at a time, and she was terrified, but she nevertheless went right to work. After explaining that the first set of movements involved learning how to imitate men riding horses in a rodeo, she demonstrated by throwing her head and body about as if she were riding a bucking bronco.

Initially many of the men reacted poorly to the demonstration, feeling what de Mille was doing didn't remotely

AARON COPLAND

By the time Agnes de Mille commissioned Aaron Copland to write the musical score for *Rodeo*, he was already an accomplished composer, teacher, and writer. He is often referred to as "America's composer," for his music conjures images of the untamed open ranges and Western frontiers of early twentieth-century America. His musical works cover a wide range of styles, from ballet and orchestral music to choral music and motion-picture scores. For more than four decades, Copland was considered America's premier composer.

Born in New York City on November 14, 1900, Copland learned to play the piano from one of his sisters and decided while still in his teens that he wanted to become a composer. In 1921 he traveled to France to study music at the Fontainebleau Schools of Music and Fine Arts. He was the first American student to study with the renowned musical coach Nadia Boulanger. When he returned to New York three years later, he received his first commission, for an organ concerto for Madame Boulanger's American appearances.

The evolution of Copland's musical style closely mirrored the times. For a while his music had a decidedly jazzy sound; soon he moved into more modernistic pieces. When the Great resemble dancing. Several left, leaving de Mille with ten to take the parts in *Rodeo*. For the next two hours, de Mille put them through a strenuous workout. "I rolled on the floor with them, lurched, contorted, jack-knifed, hung suspended and ground my teeth. They groaned and strained. I beat them out in impact, resilience, and endurance. I broke them to my handling. I broke them technically, which was where they lived and worshipped." (De Mille, *Piper*, 218)

Depression hit in 1929 and many Americans found themselves out of work, interest in abstract music waned, and Copland entered the world of dance, composing his first ballet in 1938 for the outlaw Western *Billy the Kid*. He next wrote the musical score for Agnes de Mille's *Rodeo*, and he was commissioned by Martha Graham to write one of his best-known compositions, *Appalachian Spring*. With the outbreak of World War II, Copland was asked to write some patriotic music for the Cincinnati Symphony. He produced *A Lincoln Portrait* and later *Fanfare for the Common Man*.

Although Copland is best known for his ballet and concert works, he also wrote musical scores for several Hollywood motion pictures, including *Of Mice and Men* (1939), *Our Town* (1940), *The Red Pony* (1949), and *The Heiress* (1949). He stopped composing in 1970 but remained active as a lecturer and conductor through the mid-1980s. He also wrote a number of books on music and music appreciation.

In 1964, President Lyndon B. Johnson awarded Copland the Presidential Medal of Freedom for his contribution to American artistic life. Copland died in Tarrytown, New York, on December 2, 1990, shortly after his ninetieth birthday.

Aaron Copland in his studio. Having already composed much music based on American themes, as well as the scores for ballets such as *Billy the Kid*, Aaron Copland was tailor-made to compose the music for *Rodeo*. De Mille was delighted when he agreed to work on the show and equally pleased to find that his work complemented her own. She sat with him to block almost the entire score minute by minute. The result was a major success, the first of her career.

Two days later, de Mille summoned the women. They too thought de Mille was a bit odd, but they too humored her. It took de Mille four hours to teach a boy to kiss a girl at the "dance." Many thought she was perverse and unbearable, but as time went on they began to understand, and some even began to enjoy this new style of dance. One, Frederic Franklin, impressed de Mille with his strength, technical skill, and timing, as well as his endless vitality. She came to believe Franklin was the core of the Ballet Russe, helping everyone get through the exhaustive rehearsals, performances, and endless touring. De Mille's female lead, Lubov Roudenko, continued to try to insert some moves from classical ballet; she did not succeed but was happy with her role anyway.

De Mille traveled with the troupe on the show's 1942 tour, continuing to rehearse the show in segments—scene two in San Francisco, scene three in Seattle. They traveled, rehearsed, performed, and then started all over again, sometimes staying in a city for a week, other times moving on after just one night. The whole schedule was grueling and, despite what outsiders may think, very unglamorous. Most dancers are poorly paid, have very few personal possessions, and rarely get a glimpse of life outside their tightly controlled environment.

Once back in New York after the summer tour, de Mille and the troupe rehearsed for three weeks straight, six hours a day. At last the day came for a complete show rehearsal. De Mille finally allowed an audience. In attendance were Denham; David Libidins, the Ballet Russe de Monte Carlo's business manager; musical conductor Franz Allers; Deakin; *régisseur* (stage manager) Ivan Yazvinsky; their wives; and de Mille's mother, Anna. The troupe performed the show flawlessly, prompting Denham to jump up at the end, yelling, "Thanks God, Agnes, Malinki. Thanks God. What a ballet!" (De Mille, *Piper*, 227)

With that the troupe took a three-week vacation. De Mille used the time to rehearse, since she was to dance the role of the Cowgirl on opening night. When it came, de Mille arrived at the Metropolitan Opera House at six to limber up, apply her makeup, and get into her Cowgirl costume—bow, boots, belt, hat, slacks, and shirt. Ballet Theatre also used the Opera House for its performances and its schedule overlapped with Denham's Ballet Russe de Monte Carlo. Dancers, stage crews, and directors passed one another in the halls and dressing rooms.

Ballet Theatre artistic director and choreographer Léonide Massine was present. De Mille felt the tension. Massine and Denham had had a falling out, which was what had prompted Denham to seek out a new choreographer—de Mille. Competitive rivalry and resentment permeated the air. Massine's wife came into the dressing room to chat with Ballet Theatre's star, Nathalie Krassovska. The two talked incessantly in Russian, and de Mille had no idea what their conversation was about.

When de Mille rose to leave, Mrs. Massine spoke to her, first asking if she was nervous. De Mille acknowledged that she was not only nervous, but sick to her stomach. Massine wished her good luck and success, which prompted de Mille to quietly reply, "I hope we have success. The success or failure of my life depends on the next half hour. And I hope, for the company's sake, there is success. Much depends on this ballet for them, too. If I have failed them they are in a bad way. And they have worked hard, harder than you can imagine." (De Mille, *Piper*, 230–231) In a softer tone, Massine then wished de Mille success for everyone.

For de Mille, the moment had come. The theater was sold-out. She knew many of those occupying seats, including her mother, who had never wavered in her support of her daughter's dream. De Mille joined Freddie Franklin, Robert Pagent, James Starbuck, and others on the stage behind the gold curtain. Waiting in the wings were the ladies: Maria Tallchief, Betty Low, Dorothy Etheridge, and Milada Mladova. Conductor Franz Allers gave de Mille a kiss before heading to the orchestra pit. In the next instant the orchestra came to life, loud and thunderous.

Agnes de Mille, 1952. De Mille's family was composed of overachievers in the world of theater and the creative arts, but her own choice of dance was considered taboo. Her characteristic determination would see her clearly through the many obstacles she faced in realizing her dreams—and the long years it would take to "find her feet." Her contributions to dance and choreography would extend well beyond even the broadest scope of her vision.

As the curtain began to rise, de Mille took in the enormity of what she had worked toward, and what was about to happen. "If it is possible for a life to change at one given moment, if it is possible for all movement, growth and accumulated power to become apparent at one single point, then my hour struck at 9:40, October 16, 1942. Chewing gum, squinting under a Texas hat, I turned to face what I had been preparing for the whole of my life." (De Mille, 232)

The performance seemed to move in fast-forward to de Mille, almost going too quickly. At her first exit off the stage, de Mille heard applause. It continued throughout every scene, it seemed. There was laughter, too, just as she had promised the dancers and Denham so many months ago. There were mistakes and miscues as well, but the audience didn't seem to notice or care. Caught up in the excitement of the show, much of the movement was a blur to de Mille— dancers rushed past, grabbing and releasing partners; Freddie lifted, carried, pushed, lowered de Mille. Offstage for a moment, she could hardly catch her breath before Freddie was again propelling her back onstage for more lifts, dancing, and twirling, leaving de Mille feeling like they had been shot out of a cannon.

Just as suddenly, the curtain was coming down—it was over. De Mille didn't even allow herself to savor the moment. Her mind reeled—how many mistakes had she made? How many mistakes had occurred in the maddening rush to perform? Before she could get too deep into her negative analysis, Freddie took her by the hand as the curtain rose for the company to take a bow. Flower bouquets came and came. They continued to bow. The audience clapped wildly and even called out. After the eighth curtain call, de Mille looked down and saw members of the orchestra standing and clapping. It was Freddie who told de Mille what was happening: "This is an ovation. This is the real thing. Take it." (De Mille, *Piper*, 233)

In all, *Rodeo* received twenty-two curtain calls that night. De Mille's dressing room was mobbed. Flowers filled the floor. Congratulatory telegrams arrived; the phone rang off the hook. Outside someone asked Anna if she was proud of her daughter, to which she replied that she had always been proud of her, even when no one would hire her. She went home to put up coffee and lay out pastries and wait to receive the horde of guests who wanted to share in de Mille's triumphant evening.

For de Mille, the evening was far greater than just an opening night success. Finally the window had opened, bringing in the rush of fresh air she had waited to feel for fourteen years. Like that window, the world of dance was now wide open to her.

2

De Mille's Illustrious Background

1905–1914

This is the story of an American dancer, a spoiled egocentric wealthy girl, who learned with difficulty to become a worker, to set and meet standards, to brace a Victorian sensibility to contemporary roughhousing, and who, with happy good fortune, participated by the side of great colleagues in a renaissance of the most ancient and magical of all the arts.

—Agnes de Mille

In the two decades (1920–1940) of the motion picture industry's early growth, both technologically and creatively, the name de Mille was synonymous with power and wealth. But that name referred to Cecil Blount de Mille, not his niece Agnes.

Despite being born into a family of wealth and prominence and growing up amid all the advantages enjoyed by the well-educated, the creative elite, and the social upper crust, Agnes

Henry George. Far from the world of theater and art, de Mille's maternal grandfather, Henry George, authored the economic text *Progress and Poverty*, which was surpassed in popularity in its time only by the Bible. The work, based on George's "Single Tax" theory, was the culmination of many years of hard work and sacrifice, and it earned him international recognition. De Mille chose the path of her father, uncle, and cousin: the theater. Her efforts, like her grandfather's, would eventually be rewarded.

George de Mille struggled through the first half of her life before achieving either power or wealth.

Members of the de Mille family were driven to over-achieve, and even though Uncle Cecil and Agnes's father, William, worked in the creative arts (Cecil was a very successful Hollywood director and William a moderately successful playwright and screenwriter), the one profession she desperately wanted to pursue—dance—was taboo. Even without trying to overcome the objections of her parents, Agnes faced two other major obstacles in realizing her dream—her physique and her age.

For the better part of fourteen years, Agnes traveled back and forth across the Atlantic Ocean in search of recognition and achievement in America and Europe, with minimal success. Her body was not made for the delicate style of ballet dance—her feet were too small, her bust and buttocks too large. She always seemed rather disheveled, with her mass of wild, unruly red hair. With a string of disastrous romances, and financially dependent on her mother, Anna, Agnes viewed her life as a failure, something that just didn't happen to the de Milles. By 1942, Agnes's career and future both looked bleak. There was a war raging in Europe and the Pacific, she was alone, and there were no dancing jobs on the horizon. Yet 1942 became her defining year, for she would stun the dance community and find an enduring love at last.

THE DE MILLE FAMILY, 1648–1897

Agnes George de Mille was born into a line of artistic, creative men and women who were noted for their strength and self-reliance. Her paternal grandfather, Henry Churchill de Mille (1853), was a descendant of the Dutch Episcopalian DeMils who had been in the United States since before the American Revolution, arriving in 1648. Henry's father, William, a local merchant and politician, had fought on the side of the

Confederacy during the Civil War. Agnes's grandmother, Matilda Beatrice Samuel, called Beatrice, was born in Liverpool, England, in 1853. Her father, Sylvester Samuel, a German Jewish businessman, came to America from England in 1871 with his Eastern European wife, Cecilia. They settled in Brooklyn, New York.

Beatrice Samuel gravitated toward the arts, developing a particularly strong passion for the theater. While attending a meeting at a local music and literary society, Beatrice met Henry de Mille. He, too, loved the theater; he had even written his first play while a teenager. Henry had wanted to pursue a career as a playwright, but his parents had sent him to Columbia College to study theology. He'd changed his major to education and continued to write.

Beatrice, though the daughter of Jewish immigrants, was drawn to the tall, red-headed Gentile de Mille. In those days, families discouraged marrying outside one's faith. In some Jewish families, a child who married a non-Jew was disowned. Beatrice was not deterred by the possibility, though. She and Henry were married in 1876. She even converted to his religion, solidifying her commitment.

Henry and Beatrice set up their home in Manhattan and had two sons, William Churchill (1878) and Cecil Blount (1881) de Mille. Splitting his time between teaching and writing, Henry wrote amateur plays and sometimes filled in as a reader for the Madison Square Theater. At the theater, Henry met David Belasco, an aspiring producer with terrific business acumen. Each man's talents complemented the other's — Henry writing plays, and Belasco directing them.

Though happy with his commercial success, Henry longed for the kind of recognition reserved for serious play- wrights. He finally achieved it for his 1891 adaptation of German writer Ludwig Fulda's drama *The Lost Paradise*. Not only did the recognition come, but so did financial security. Additions to the de Mille family included daughter

Agnes Beatrice and a three-story Victorian-style home built on seventy-six acres of land Henry purchased in Pompton Lakes, New Jersey.

The family's bliss was shattered just two years later, at the first Christmas at Pompton Lakes. Henry died shortly after contracting typhoid fever. Suddenly widowed with three children (William was fourteen, Cecil eleven, Agnes barely two) and with no money, forty-year-old Beatrice exploited her love of theater and her knowledge of education to support her family. In an era where a woman's role was as wife and home-maker, Beatrice again defied convention by opening a school for girls in her home and becoming a playwright agent.

With an office on Broadway, Beatrice used her steely determination to break through the male-dominated industry and built an impressive client list by carving out her own niche—representing female playwrights. She did have difficulty balancing family and two businesses—the girls' school floundered, but the writer representation business flourished. Despite another devastating death—daughter Agnes died of spinal meningitis just two years after Henry— Beatrice proved resilient.

William received some schooling in Freiburg, Germany, before returning to New York and enrolling at Columbia University. Cecil was completing his pre-college schooling at a military academy in Pennsylvania. William took full advantage of what Columbia had to offer. A true son of Henry and Beatrice, Henry was drawn to the theater, particularly writing. Besides his love of writing, he was quite athletic, participating in track, fencing, boxing, and tennis. Despite Henry's deathbed wish that his sons not pursue careers in the theater, when William signed up for a playwrighting class, he was hooked. After college, William (and later Cecil) studied at the American Academy of Dramatic Arts. Eventually, both of Henry de Mille's sons made the theater, and later the motion picture industry, their life's work.

THE GEORGE FAMILY, 1839–1897

The maternal side of Agnes George de Mille's family tree was no less colorful than her father's. The Georges were recognized not for their involvement in the theater, but for a passion for political economics. Agnes's maternal grandfather, Henry George (1839–1897), was a rather radical fellow for his time. From the age of thirteen, when he dropped out of school and left his home in Philadelphia, he had supported himself in various jobs—errand boy, cabin boy (he made a complete voyage around the world), typesetter, printer. Henry was a voracious reader and began developing his own ideas about economics, from which his "Single Tax" doctrine was born.

When Henry was about twenty-one, he married seventeen-year-old Annie Corsina Fox, an Irish-Catholic girl who had grown up in Australia. Annie's parents did not think Henry was a suitable husband for their daughter, since he had no money or immediate means to support her. Because of their objections, the young couple eloped. They eventually settled in San Francisco, California, where Henry worked as a journeyman printer.

Fascinated by a world in which poverty existed simultaneously alongside affluence and leisure, Henry wanted to discover why they occurred in tandem. In his free time, Henry wrote his economics bible, *Progress and Poverty* (1879). He proposed in his "Single Tax" theory to abolish all taxes except the tax levied on the value of land. George explained his rationale for his "Single Tax" theory this way:

> When we tax houses, crops, money, furniture, capital, or wealth in any of its forms, we take from individuals what rightfully belongs to them. We violate the right of property, and in the name of the state commit robbery. But when we tax ground values, we take from individuals what does not belong to them, but belongs to the community, and which cannot be left to individuals without the robbery of other individuals. (De Mille, *Speak to Me*, 388)

While Henry worked on writing *Progress and Poverty*, his finances barely covered the family's basic needs. With the birth of their daughter Anna in 1877, Annie George had four children to feed and clothe. It took two more years before *Progress and Poverty* was completed and published. The book would go on to become a classic, but it was still quite a while before their living situation improved. For a time Henry took a job at a New York newspaper, leaving Annie alone in San

CECIL B. DE MILLE

His name on a movie theater marquee was as big a draw as many of the stars who appeared in his films. To his generation, Cecil B. de Mille was the quintessential producer/ director. He fit the image exactly: He wore puttees, or leather leggings secured by a strap or catch or by laces, and a beret, and he liked to have on hand the tools of his profession—a megaphone, a viewfinder (for use in choosing a camera lens), and a light meter. He was also a great storyteller and translated that talent to his films.

De Mille, born on August 12, 1881, was one of the most successful directors of Hollywood's early years because— unlike many others—he was able to make the transition from the silent-film era to the era of "talkies," or films with sound. He became known for his epic biblical creations, including *King of Kings* (1927), *Samson and Delilah* (1949), and the blockbuster spectacle *The Ten Commandments*, which he made in 1923 and again in 1956.

It is not surprising that de Mille chose to go into entertainment; he came from a theatrical family. His father, Henry, though a clergyman, wrote several plays. His mother, Beatrice, ran a traveling theatrical troupe. His older brother, William, was a student at the American Academy of Dramatic Arts in New York

Francisco with the children. To help with the finances, she ran a boarding school.

Life for the Georges had improved dramatically by 1881. Henry was able to bring his family to join him in New York, because *Progress and Poverty* had become wildly popular. Sales of his book earned Henry George international recognition and financial security. In the 1880s, *Progress and Poverty* was the second highest-selling book worldwide, eclipsed in

City. De Mille learned his trade as an actor, stage manager, and playwright (with William) under the guidance of the famed impresario David Belasco.

De Mille eventually traveled west to California, joining creative forces with the cinematic pioneers Jesse Lasky and Samuel Goldfish (later Goldwyn) in 1913. Together they formed the Jesse L. Lasky Feature Play Company, which was the precursor to Paramount Pictures. Their first film venture was a feature-length version of the play *The Squaw Man* in 1914. It was a great success and helped to launch all three men in their careers in the motion picture industry.

De Mille either discovered or created many stars, including Gloria Swanson. In all, he produced and directed seventy films, some of which helped to solidify the careers of Claudette Colbert, Charlton Heston, and other notable actors.

Ever the showman, from 1936 until 1945 de Mille hosted and directed *Lux Radio Theatre*, which brought the actors and stories of several motion pictures to the airwaves. Though celebrated and successful himself, de Mille never thought much of his niece's talent at dancing, and he did little to help Agnes de Mille in her career.

sales only by the Bible. Henry George had many admirers, including Russian novelist Leo Tolstoy, educator John Dewey, and Henry Churchill de Mille.

It wasn't long before the Georges and the de Milles became friends, and they remained so until Henry de Mille's premature death. Both families resided in Manhattan's Greenwich Village neighborhood, and their children attended the Horace Mann School on University Place. When Anna George was eleven years old, she boldly proposed marriage to twelve-year-old William de Mille. Of course, the adolescent de Mille declined, but he and Anna stayed on friendly terms.

With the success of *Progress and Poverty,* Henry George enjoyed enormous popularity and recognition. Years later, in her biography of her father, the younger Anna had only good things to say about him. She also had an idyllic view of her parents' marriage, and so it was a devastating emotional blow to the entire family when fifty-eight-year-old Henry died suddenly of a heart attack in 1897. Anna was twenty years old, and she was already self-sufficient and fiercely independent.

Anna's piercing blue eyes, waist-length golden-red hair, and feminine demeanor were attributes enough to attract many suitors, but she had adored William since before she had proposed to him nine years earlier. Along the way William had grown quite fond of Anna, too, expressing his fondness by giving her his class ring. Officially engaged in 1902, they had to endure being apart during the week while William taught fencing classes at Pompton Lakes and Anna remained at home with her mother in New York. Though they saw each other on weekends, William wrote to Anna often, expressing his love and longing for the time when they would be together forever.

The marriage of Anna George and William Churchill de Mille took place on March 30, 1903. The two appeared to be deeply devoted to one another. Anna thought her bridegroom a genius; William thought his wife an angel. For a while the newlyweds lived in the attic studio of Beatrice de Mille's boarding school. William continued to write and got his first big break with his play *Strongheart*. Separated from his new bride again while the play toured successfully around the country for much of 1904, William returned home a triumphant playwright at the tender age of twenty-five. The de Milles were now able to move from William's mother's house to a small apartment on Morningside Park.

AGNES DE MILLE'S EARLY YEARS

On September 18, 1905, at 357 West 118th Street in the predominantly white middle-class neighborhood of Harlem, Anna gave birth at home to a daughter she and William named Agnes George de Mille. Little Agnes enjoyed a rather comfortable early childhood. William continued to write a string of successful plays and was able to afford some additional comforts for his family. Anna enjoyed the benefit of having live-in help from a cook and nurse.

Three years after Agnes's birth, her sister, Margaret George, was born. According to de Mille, their childhood was typical: "Margaret and I passed our first years in the exact routine of New York children—head colds, walks in the park, curtailment of racing and screaming in the apartment." (De Mille, *Piper*, 10) Summers were spent at the Georges' huge compound near the Catskill Mountains at the borders of New York State, New Jersey, and Pennsylvania. Merriewold, as the 2,000-acre property was called, had several buildings that had been built by the Georges over time. When Agnes was four, William bought a cottage for his family and over time acquired an additional thirty acres.

Agnes loved spending time at Merriewold, wandering freely around the grounds of the country estate, bonding with nature. There were all kinds of animals in the woods— deer, raccoons, and beavers—that were never seen in Harlem, and they fascinated Agnes. She learned to recognize a variety of flowers and enjoyed the occasional privilege of going along on a sunset canoe ride with her parents. She loved the peacefulness that was so different from life in the city. "My hair got redder. I moved directly, like an animal. I was quiet. I listened. . . . You heard with your skin; you breathed light and shade." (Easton, 15)

Agnes's family and surroundings were what kept her universe balanced. Despite being a curious, very bright, creative child, she also had an aggressive, at times almost overpowering, personality. An attractive adolescent, Agnes had her mother's blue eyes, a thick mane of curly red hair, and a freckled face. The boys she liked did not reciprocate her feelings, often leaving her feeling quite lonely. To compensate, Agnes made up an abundance of imaginary companions who romped through the woods and played a variety of imaginative games with her.

Anna and the girls stayed at Merriewold through the summer season, returning to New York City in September. When not on business in New York, William stayed at Merriewold, too, where he could be with his beloved wife and his "little fellers," as he affectionately called his daughters, Agnes and Margaret. The more successful William became, the more his work took him away from Anna and the girls. But he wrote often, sending letters and cards to his daughters as well as to Anna. Occasionally, William sent gifts that were delivered with huge expressions of love.

FROM HARLEM TO HOLLYWOOD

At summer's end the de Milles packed up and headed back to New York City. In 1911, Agnes was enrolled at the Horace Mann School, the same educational institution that had been attended by her parents. Life continued rather routinely for a while—William had been on a roll with hit plays, including *The Genius* (1906), *Classmates* (1907), *The Warrens of Virginia* (1907), and *The Woman* (1911). Often actors and actresses

William and Cecil B. de Mille. Despite Henry de Mille's wishes that his sons not pursue careers in the theater, both Cecil B. and William, Agnes's father (at left), did just that. William's career as a playwright was steady and successful. Cecil struggled a bit at first but finally found immense success as a pioneer in the emerging medium of motion pictures. This photograph of the brothers was taken in Hollywood around 1915.

visited the de Mille house. Agnes marveled at the grace, sophistication, and style of the women, and the dapper, smartly dressed men who called on her father and mother.

In 1914, when her father's brother, Cecil, shifted away from his fluctuating writing and acting career, nine-year-old Agnes could not have foreseen the routine of her life coming to an end—the end of summers at Merriewold and winters in New York City with guests coming and going in a rhythmic flow to and from her house. Though the motion picture industry was in its infancy—films were only seven or eight minutes long— Cecil and two friends, Jesse Lasky and Samuel Goldfish (later changed to Goldwyn), pooled their talents to attempt to produce the first full-length feature film. Instead of working in New Jersey, where most movie production was taking place, the three headed west, where the weather was warmer and land was less expensive.

William thought his brother's latest venture was folly. Cecil didn't care. Of the two, he was much more of a risk-taker. Eventually, Cecil, Lasky, and Goldfish settled in the undeveloped town of Hollywood, California. They rented a barn, set up a workspace, and in a little more than six weeks produced the film *The Squaw Man*, the first feature-length motion picture in California. The movie was a commercial success and was booked for screenings across the country.

William was stunned when he saw his brother's film for the first time, and later said, "I saw unrolled before my eyes the first really new form of dramatic story-telling which had been invented for some 500 years." (Easton, 21) Cecil tried to convince his brother that a whole new writing career awaited him in California—film producers needed screenwriters. William resisted, despite the fact that he no longer felt inspired to write for the stage. By the age of thirty-six, he had lost the inner excitement he used to experience when creating a new work. Only after his latest play, *After Five* (1913), opened to a less than receptive audience did William acquiesce.

Persuaded to give screenwriting a try in California, William left Anna and the girls behind and headed for Hollywood. It took William less than a week to embrace his new environment.

He felt alive again, rejuvenated by the energy and excitement generated by the people around him, who were also enthusiastic about being part of the new motion picture industry. He wrote to Anna, telling her of the beauty of the untouched wilderness, the numerous orange groves, and the open roads. He also told her that he felt home for him was where she and the girls were and he longed to have them reunited as a family. In a letter dated October 17, 1914, William wrote in more urgent tones, "GET THE STUFF IN STORAGE AND COME TO ME." (Easton, 22)

Agnes couldn't even imagine what things would look like at the other end of the country, but her genes had been infused with a sense of adventure long before birth. Still, one can also imagine a slightly anxious nine-year-old Agnes taking one last look around before boarding the train, as if trying to burn the images into her memory forever. Would she ever wander around the grounds at her beloved Merriewold again? Would she ever see New York again?

Transformed by a Ballerina

1914–1919

Anna Pavlova! My life stops as I write that name. . . . I had witnessed the power of beauty, and in some chamber of my heart I lost forever my irresponsibility.

—Agnes de Mille, *Dance to the Piper*

Before he headed west with partners Jesse Lasky and Samuel Goldfish in 1913 to start their film company, Cecil B. de Mille asked his brother for $5,000. William had lent Cecil money for many other ventures that had failed; this time, he politely refused. Had William funded his brother one more time, though, he would have ended up with a nice percentage of interest in what would later become the multimillion-dollar mega-studio Paramount Pictures, Inc.

Despite the lack of financial support from his brother, Cecil saw great opportunities for William in California. The

The incomparable Anna Pavlova. For Agnes de Mille, the Russian prima ballerina Anna Pavlova (1881–1931) embodied all a person could aspire to be. De Mille was thirteen years old the first time she saw Pavlova perform, and the experience affected her profoundly enough to set the course of her destiny. Pavlova, who had worked for Sergey Diaghilev, inspired de Mille's commitment to the art of dance. De Mille would follow in her footsteps by helping to popularize ballet in the United States.

film industry was growing fast, and so was the area called Hollywood. Cecil knew that his talented brother would have tremendous prospects in dramatic writing for the new medium. When *After Five* opened to a lukewarm reception,

William no longer needed coaxing from Cecil to join him in California. William went west, and he enjoyed the change in environment, both geographically and creatively.

In a letter to Anna, William wrote, "This particular art is *really* in its infancy. . . . This is the one company with which I can work unfettered and really have the opportunity to rise quickly to the very top." (Easton, 21) William also found that the Los Angeles area, where Hollywood was located, had much to offer—a pleasant climate, undisturbed desert, a colorful mountain range, endless stretches of orange and olive groves, and the blue waters of the Pacific Ocean nearby. The newness and the refreshing atmosphere made William feel young again, and he looked forward to sharing the experience with his wife and daughters.

On the train during the journey west, Agnes peered from the window of her Pullman car as it traveled through endless miles of open wilderness and beautiful orange and red mountain formations. Occasionally, she glimpsed American Indians riding bareback in the distance. She hoped she'd go to school with Native Americans and have her very own horse so she could ride with the cowboys. She grew excited at the mere thought that she could be in the movies.

AN INTRODUCTION TO HOLLYWOOD

Agnes was a bit disappointed when she arrived in Los Angeles and saw that it was just a rural town. There were palm trees instead of stately maple and chestnut trees. There were mountains, but they were nowhere near as majestic and colorful as the ones she'd seen on the train ride through Arizona. There were no Native Americans in sight, just plain-looking folks. Hollywood Boulevard, the main thoroughfare through town, was the only paved road. The population of only 7,500 people was a far cry from the enormous population of crowded New York City.

Having the family reunited was the most important thing

to Agnes, though, and that made up for any disappointment she might have felt about her new surroundings. The de Mille family settled into a modest home at 1814 Hillcrest Road, at the foot of a hill that backed up to open wilderness. The grounds were smaller than those at Merriewold, but there was still plenty of room for the de Mille girls to run freely. Agnes and Margaret were enrolled in the Hollywood School for Girls. Like those at the Horace Mann School, classes were held outside, but in a garden area instead of on the roof of the school. Classmates included Joel McCrea and Douglas Fairbanks, Jr., who would later become successful motion picture stars, and Edith and Irene Mayer, daughters of soon-to-be-famous studio mogul Louis B. Mayer.

The motion picture studio, a converted stable on Vine Street, looked out of place amid the beautiful pepper trees whose feathery palm leaves hung down on either side of the street. Uncle Cecil's "studio" was a dull, dark green, wooden building stained with the residue of the pepper tree bark. The studio, within easy walking distance of the de Mille home, was conveniently located for Agnes's father. Often in the early evening Agnes saw her father and uncle walking across the vacant lot, silhouetted by a beautiful, fiery red sunset.

William's writing flourished in his new environment. He turned out nine screenplays in his first full year of writing for this curious new art form. The film creation process was quick. A full-length feature could be shot and wrapped within two weeks' time. Allowing a week up front for preparations such as script revisions, construction of sets, and rehearsals, and a week for editing and cutting, a film could be released for screenings in about one month.

In those days of the film industry's infancy, it was not unusual for a film shoot to be observed by studio employees or a gallery of Hollywood's young residents, who gathered in those backyards that offered a bird's-eye view of the process. If Cecil was shooting a really spectacular scene, such as tossing actress Gloria Swanson into a pit of lions or burning Geraldine Ferrar at the stake for *Joan the Woman* (1917), members of the cast and crew's families might come to the set to watch up close.

Young Agnes was completely entranced by the costumes, makeup, sets, acting, and filming process. At home, she copied what she'd seen while on the set, pretending to direct her own productions with some of the other girls in the neighborhood.

Most of the kids in the area had parents who were the empire builders of the motion picture industry—the Goldwyns, Mayers, Laskys, Selznicks, and Zukors. They were aware of whose relatives worked for whom, and they were fiercely loyal to the companies employing their parents, producing plenty of competitive posturing at school. Agnes found most of her classmates' constant one-upmanship maddening. She noticed that one girl, Mary Hunter, the niece of writer Mary Austin, didn't seem intimidated by all the fame and competition around her. The two became best friends and remained so throughout their lives.

The class Agnes enjoyed the most was pantomime. She especially liked dancing and idolized Geraldine Ferrar, desperately wanting to be like her and act in the movies. Despite the fact that making motion pictures was a family business, a career in acting or dancing was not what William had in mind for his elder daughter. Agnes's life was instead filled with more "acceptable" activities like French lessons, piano lessons, swimming lessons, tennis, homework, painting, sewing, listening to music, reading—everything *but* acting and dancing.

She thought her father a genius and did anything to please him, to make him proud of her:

He was an excellent photographer; I learned photography. He sang well and half-joking suggested that I learn the piano in order to accompany him; my response ran to five hours' daily practicing in the summer and full-length recitals with my sister. . . . He played brilliant tennis. . . . I tried to learn tennis, making the semifinals always in the junior tournaments. He told me what to read; I read. . . . He told me to write. I became editor of the school paper. (De Mille, *Piper*, 29)

When it came to acting or dance, though, William remained firm. He did not want his daughters involved in the theater. He wanted his daughters to be refined, well-mannered, bright, intelligent women, and he was bent on having them raised that way.

Agnes wanted to walk on a studio set, dressed in an extravagant costume, and release all emotion within her in a perfect scene. She wanted to burst through the fields, dancing, jumping, and twirling, in constant motion in the wide-open expanse without any constraints. What Anna and William may not have realized was that they were raising Agnes in a way that went against every aspect of her very nature.

ANNA PAVLOVA

Anna de Mille certainly enjoyed many of the artistic activities in which the family was engaged. She particularly liked the theater and music, and she often played the mechanical organ in the evenings during "family time." Agnes rarely sat still whenever she heard music and frequently danced, as most little girls do, just to enjoy the freedom of moving and to garner attention.

When the girls were old enough, Anna took them along when she attended an opera or ballet. When Agnes was five, Anna took her to see a performance that featured the Danish ballerina Adeline Genée. The experience inspired Agnes to enlist the participation of other children and put on her own dance pageants at Merriewold. At that time, though, dance for the young Agnes was just whimsy and child's play.

When she was thirteen, she saw a performance by Anna

Pavlova and was immediately mesmerized by the delicate movements of the petite Russian prima ballerina. Agnes described what she saw in *Dance to the Piper*:

> All her gestures were liquid and possessed of an inner rhythm that flowed to inevitable completion with the finality of architecture or music. Her arms seemed to lift not from the elbow or the arm socket, but from the base of her spine. Her legs seemed to function from the waist. When she bent her head her whole spine moved and the motion was completed the length of the arm through the elongation of her slender hand and the quivering reaching fingers. (De Mille, *Piper*, 40)

Watching Pavlova so affected Agnes that even years later she wrote that she had seen only two dancers as great—Alicia Markova and Margot Fonteyn. There were others who had

ANNA PAVLOVA

The mere mention of the name Anna Pavlova conjures up the image of the graceful "Dying Swan" solo she performed to the music of the French composer Camille Saint-Saens's *Carnival of the Animals*. Arranged for her by the great Russian choreographer Mikhail Fokine in 1907, "Dying Swan" became Pavlova's signature solo. It was just one of the performances that earned Pavlova her place among the legendary ballerinas of the twentieth century.

Pavlova was born into poverty in the Russian city of St. Petersburg in 1881 and began attending the Imperial Ballet Academy at the age of ten. By the time she graduated in 1899 there was a refined and poetic style to her dancing that impressed both her teachers and dance critics. She joined the Maryinsky Theatre as second soloist in 1902, kicked higher, balanced longer, or turned faster than Pavlova, but to Agnes physical technique didn't rate as high as the ability to express passion. In Pavlova, Agnes saw "an intoxicated rapture, a focus of energy, Dionysian in its physical intensity" (De Mille, *Piper*, 40) that she never saw equaled by a performer on any stage in the world.

Thirteen-year-old Agnes knew what her destiny was the moment she saw Pavlova finish her last motion in her ballet — to become a dancer. Once home, Agnes begged her parents to allow her to take ballet lessons, to no avail. She continued to pursue her intense interest by learning everything she could about dancing, through reading and by carefully poring over endless photographs. Agnes even created a scrapbook of photos of dancers.

When the Diaghilev Ballets Russes came to Los Angeles, Anna took Agnes and Margaret to see a Saturday matinee

and by 1906 she had earned the title of prima ballerina.

Pavlova performed across Europe, making occasional appearances with Sergey Diaghilev's Ballets Russes. Eventually, she formed her own dance company and toured the world, including the United States, presenting ballet performances including *pas de deux* (duets) with a partner and a *corps de ballet* (ensemble). In her solos, Pavlova would portray a bird, a dragonfly, and, of course, her signature swan.

Pavlova maintained a hectic and extensive schedule, performing almost to the point of exhaustion, until her death of pneumonia in 1931. Considered a genius by audiences and colleagues alike, Anna Pavlova is credited with popularizing ballet in America, as well as inspiring countless young dancers around the world with her characteristic grace and unique style.

performance of *La Sylphide*, a "romantic reverie" set to the music of Frédéric Chopin. There were other afternoon matinee excursions, but when the shows were over and Anna's friends had finished their last sip of tea over discussions about what they'd seen—when the props, sets, and costumes from the backyard pageants were all packed away—Agnes was left with only the empty desire to be a performer. She listened nightly as her father talked of his work, desperate to be a part of the profession in the grown-ups' world.

A glimmer of hope for Agnes's aspirations arrived when Denishawn Company cofounder and dance teacher Ruth St. Denis visited the de Mille home. Agnes performed one of St. Denis's dances for her, and St. Denis was impressed enough that she told Anna to begin Agnes's training at once. William again politely rebuffed the suggestion, even though St. Denis and her husband, Ted Shawn, became close friends of William and Anna. Agnes was finally able to break through her father's resistance to lessons when doctors discovered that Margaret had fallen arches in her feet, and her orthopedist offered the best remedy—ballet dancing!

TO DANCE AT LAST

Though there was nothing wrong with Agnes's feet, William didn't want to be accused of favoritism, so he permitted both girls to take ballet lessons. Anna enrolled Agnes and Margaret into the Theodore Kosloff School of Imperial Russian Ballet. Trained at the Moscow Imperial School, Theodore Kosloff had been a member of the original Diaghilev Ballets Russes and performed with Bronislava Nijinsky and Tamara Karsavina. As a professional courtesy to Cecil, Kosloff agreed to take the de Mille sisters as pupils without accepting any payment for the duration of Agnes's and Margaret's lessons.

Though thrilled to be taking lessons at last, Agnes was quickly stung by Kosloff's initial assessment of her suitability as a dancer. He told her that her knees were weak, her spine was

The Pacific Ocean, Hollywood, 1913. While William de Mille's career began to lose momentum, his brother's ventures in motion pictures promised brilliant success. William finally followed his brother's increasingly attractive invitations and moved to the budding town of Los Angeles, where he sought inspiration in the vast, open Pacific coastline. Agnes and the rest of the family would soon follow, leaving behind the rhythm and culture of New York City for new adventures in the West. The Western spirit would find its way into Agnes de Mille's choreography years later.

curved, she was a bit heavy for her age, and she was rather old to begin training. Despite the less-than-promising evaluation, Agnes had her mother purchase the necessary toe shoes and attire for her first lesson.

Teacher Miss Fredova (Winifred Edwards), a former student of Anna Pavlova, showed Agnes how to use the barre and bend her knees deeply in *plié*. The exercise continued with Fredova chanting, "Down-ee, two-ee, three-ee, four-ee, Nuca. Give me this fourth position. Repeat the exercise." (De Mille, *Piper*, 47)

Agnes began each lesson the same way and always practiced exactly the same way. These exercises, though tedious and boring, strengthened her leg and thigh muscles. It was the secret key to successful dancing, and Agnes approached every moment with the passion of a professional. She soon learned how much her body could hurt and how exhausting ballet could be. Most importantly, Agnes learned that no one ever sat down and rested. She learned how to rest her insteps by lying on her back and pressing her feet flat up against the wall, how to bind up her toes so they wouldn't bleed through her ballet shoes, how to overcome exhaustion through mental toughness—and she learned never to miss daily practice, no matter what.

Despite her psychological and emotional desire to excel as a dancer, she just couldn't overcome the limitations of her physique. The ideal shape for a ballet dancer is a long-limbed body with a small torso. Agnes was not blessed with such a body. She had a long torso, and her arms and legs were short. Neither did she have the high, tight instep and wide stretch in her Achilles tendon, the most important tendon in a dancer's body. It is the Achilles tendon that provides the spring when a dancer pushes off when executing a jump and cushions the blow when the foot lands.

The shortcomings of Agnes's physical makeup were more than compensated by an incredible endurance. Still, at fourteen, it was little consolation. Her parents' restrictions made things even more difficult. They limited Agnes to one private lesson of forty-five minutes and one hour-long class lesson a week, while the rest of the students attended every day and practiced together. Agnes insisted on practicing at home. Her mother had a makeshift barre installed in their bathroom and limited her home practice to forty minutes a day. With no mirror, no proper floor, and no accompanying music, Agnes was still at an incredible disadvantage.

Dance didn't get any easier for Agnes despite the fact that

she worked harder and harder, pushing herself and punishing her body in order to make up for the lack of instruction time. She came to believe that she was the worst pupil in her class, and that was hard to swallow. All her life, Agnes had believed she was destined for greatness—she certainly had excelled at everything she'd tried. The de Mille and George women weren't quitters, though; they were strong, self-sufficient, and gifted in their own ways. Having come this far and this close to working toward her passion to become a dancer, Agnes was not about to give in—to her parents, her teachers, or her classmates. She certainly wasn't going to give up on herself.

The Long Search for Success

1919–1927

Who am I? the artist asks. And he devotes his whole life to finding out.
—Agnes de Mille

Though she wasn't the most talented student, or the most physically suited to dancing ballet, Agnes had enough passion to fuel her drive to excel despite the obstacles in her way. One of the biggest obstacles she had to overcome was her father's contempt for the discipline. "My father, like all educated men, considered dancing at best exhibitionistic acrobatics, and certainly a field that offered neither intellectual nor spiritual challenge," de Mille wrote in *Dance to the Piper*. (59–60)

Having taken lessons, Agnes understood the sacrifices dancers made to devote all of their energy to studying and practicing the discipline. She also recognized that the dance

Ballet Class. Despite her father's strong determination to see his daughters not involved in the theater, Agnes and her sister began to study dance. It would be nine years, though, before Agnes de Mille would even begin performing professionally. Success would take even longer to come. This undated photograph was taken when de Mille was performing the innovative *Ballet Class* (1927), one of her earliest pieces.

world demanded an all-encompassing life commitment that left room for little else, including romantic or even platonic relationships. Successful dancers were "married" to their work—dance was their life, their love, and their constant companion. It was a lonely life.

William never came right out and forbade his daughter to continue with her chosen career, but he never supported her work, and at every opportunity made it clear to Agnes what he thought of her choice—he refused to attend her classes or any of her performances or engage in any conversation about activities at the Kosloff School. Knowing she would never receive his support or approval was devastating to the teenage Agnes, who idolized and adored her father.

Agnes at the time was impressionable and at times overly sensitive, and she often experienced tremendous swings of emotion. Denied her father's approval, she found solace in her schoolwork, reading, and extracurricular activities. At the same time, she felt so passionate about dance that she sometimes thought she would burst. When her idol, Anna Pavlova, came back to town for a series of performances, Agnes was filled with both excitement and dread. Certainly, her mother would take her to see Pavlova—but would she be as Agnes remembered her? What if Pavlova wasn't really so extraordinary and had just *seemed* so to a younger, less knowledgeable Agnes?

Agnes need not have worried. From the moment Pavlova stepped onstage, Agnes was transfixed once again by her beauty and grace. The ballet was *Autumn Leaves*, composed by Pavlova herself and set to the music of Frédéric Chopin. So mesmerized was Agnes that she was barely aware of Pavlova's brief departures from the stage throughout the program.

Something happened that day that was even more extraordinary than seeing Pavlova's performance. A friend tapped Agnes on the shoulder at the conclusion of the show and invited her to go backstage and *meet* Pavlova.

Backstage, people milled around all over the place. When Agnes entered Pavlova's dressing room, her idol was still in full costume, talking to some friends. Pavlova moved toward Agnes and the rest of the group to greet them. Soon Pavlova, Agnes's inspiration, her idol, was standing right in front of her, larger than life. Agnes's friend introduced her as Kosloff's best pupil, and Agnes froze. Pavlova congratulated Agnes, grabbed a bunch of flowers from a nearby basket, and handed them to her, then bent down to kiss her lightly on the cheek. Agnes was so completely overcome by the moment that she began to weep. She later remembered little after that except being escorted to a car waiting to take her home.

Once home, Agnes was more inspired than ever. She kept the flowers Pavlova had given her for ten years, safely tucked away in a box. It didn't matter to Agnes when, years later, she learned that Pavlova gave flowers to all the little girls who were brought backstage to meet her. To Agnes, Pavlova was the ambassador for ballet to little girls around the world. As Agnes got older and her own knowledge of ballet increased, she watched Pavlova's performances with a much more discerning eye. It didn't matter. Pavlova was the quintessential queen of ballet and remained so until her premature death in 1931 from double pneumonia. Of her passing de Mille wrote, "It mattered not that I had only spoken to her once and that my work lay in a different direction. She was the vision and the impulse and the goal." (De Mille, *Piper*, 66)

TO DANCE OR NOT TO DANCE

Agnes went through a lonely, insecure adolescence. Puberty transformed her from a cute child with small, defined features and smooth white skin into a teen with a thick mane of wild, curly red hair, ruddy skin, and a large nose similar to her father's, which he called "aristocratic." Her body filled out, becoming bosomy and large-hipped, making her look anything but petite. She felt uneasy and uncomfortable around most boys her age, finding them intellectually weak and less cultured than she was; she sat alone at countless dances because of this and dreaded attending them. She tended her wounded pride by telling herself that one day she'd be a famous dancer and men would fall at her feet.

The de Mille house was actually a stimulating, entertaining place to be during Agnes's teen years. William was doing well in the film business, writing screenplays and even doing some directing. His work put him in the company of some of the biggest names in Hollywood. Anna had links to the musical and

MARTHA GRAHAM

Martha Graham, often referred to as the "mother of modern dance," believed she had answered a higher calling in her career. Her impassioned mission, she believed, was to map out the path of the heart through movement. "That driving force of God that plunges through me is what I live for," she once wrote. (Long, 56) By making a complete departure from the movements and styles of classical ballet through her own groundbreaking ideas of dance, Graham created a whole new art form. In a career that spanned more than five decades, she tirelessly pursued her creative vision, amassing a legacy of 180 choreographed works.

Graham was born in Pennsylvania in 1894. She didn't see her first dance performance until she was in her late teen years—but then she was enthralled by a recital given by the ballet pioneer Ruth St. Denis. Graham joined the Denishawn School and dance troupe that St. Denis had founded with her husband, and at the very late age of twenty-two, she began her career in dance. When at last she felt a need to strike out on her own, she left the Denishawn School and moved to New York, taking a teaching job at the Eastman School of Theater. During that time she developed her own unique style of dance and began to give solo recitals.

In 1929, Graham founded the Martha Graham School of Contemporary Dance and launched a new style of dance, one literary elite. It was not uncommon for Charlie Chaplin or Douglas Fairbanks to visit. Anna often invited concert artists to her home, such as opera singer Rosa Ponselle and violinist Efrem Zimbalist. Literary guests included novelists Somerset Maugham, Rebecca West, and Michael Arlen.

that emphasized the tightening and release of the torso. Initially, audiences rejected the style, finding it jarring and ugly in comparison to the graceful, fluid movements they were accustomed to seeing in ballet performances. Graham was not bothered by this, for she believed her job was to look *interesting* in her craft—but not necessarily *beautiful*.

Graham firmly made her mark in modern dance in the 1940s, producing a body of works that have been described as "angst-ridden dance dramas—enacted on symbol-strewn sets designed by the sculptor Isamu Noguchi and accompanied by scores commissioned from such noted composers as Aaron Copland and Samuel Barber. . . ." (Long, 200)

Through her imposing presence, unwavering determination, and astounding talent, Martha Graham was able to establish modern dance as a compelling art form, one that audiences of today take seriously. She continued to perform her many original works well into her later years and to choreograph until her death at the age of ninety-six. Graham's own description of her art captures not only its power but also its intensely personal nature: "There is a vitality, a life-force, an energy, a quickening that is translated through you into action. And because there is only one of you in all of time, this expression is unique. . . ." (Golden, 156)

Aside from being a meeting place for an eclectic range of guests, the de Mille house was Anna's pride and joy, a comfortable, old-fashioned home situated on five sprawling acres amid a beautiful garden. In her book *Dance to the Piper*, Agnes gave a vivid description:

> We had the largest collection of bulbs in Southern California. Every Easter we filled clothesbaskets of white iris for our church. In July the agapanthus stood six deep in solid borders the length of the driveway and the whole space was redolent with hot lavender, broom and amaryllis and the wonderful swooning smell of the camphor trees. We had an English spring that bloomed nowhere else on our side of the Rocky Mountains, hawthorn, primroses, bluebells, violets, narcissus, grape-hyacinth, apple, quince, cherry. Many a homesick Englishman has stood silent before those beds until mother led him in to tea. (De Mille, *Piper*, 69)

Despite William's fame, Anna was really the heart and soul of the de Mille home. Aspiring artists, writers, Single Taxers, women interested in forming community clubs—they all came through Anna George de Mille's parlor.

Surrounded by a wealth of talent from a variety of disciplines, Agnes received almost constant artistic and intellectual stimulation. The one drawback for Agnes was that it became more difficult for her to find the time and place to practice her ballet without distraction. She also dreaded the lonely, boring practice, made more acute by her feeling that her technical skills had not really improved. She began questioning what future, if any, dance could hold for her. There weren't even any ballet companies in the United States.

As Agnes neared the end of high school, dancing came to mean only endless practice and exhaustion. Following graduation in 1922, she spent much of the summer thinking about her future. Toward the end of the summer she reached a decision—she would give up dance and go to college. Not surprisingly, William was delighted with his daughter's announcement.

UCLA AND THE RETURN TO DANCE

Wanting to spread her wings away from Anna and William, Agnes planned to attend Mills College in northern California. Of course, Anna would allow no such thing, and she advised her daughter that the University of California at Los Angeles (UCLA) was a perfectly fine choice and within walking distance of the house. Agnes, used to being one of only nine students in her high school class, found UCLA enormously exciting. She approached college with the same intensity she had applied to dance, going from dance artist to university scholar. Agnes signed up for more courses than was permitted and was "intoxicated by all the learning available." (De Mille, *Piper*, 74)

Agnes chose English as her major and pursued writing while studying poetry and literature. In her freshman year, she worked at her studies incessantly, never attending a football game, a school dance, or a sorority tea. Her social life consisted of occasional teas with members of the English department faculty, including Dr. Lily Bess Campbell, and a few dates. When Agnes fell in love with Alfred Longueil, her poetry professor, an alarmed Anna de Mille enrolled in the class to keep the situation under her watchful eye.

In her sophomore year, Agnes started driving to campus in a used Buick that William had given to her. Definitely her mother's daughter, Agnes always arrived late for classes and appointments. She often fell asleep during afternoon lectures and had grave difficulty learning to think creatively on demand. For most of the allotted time given for an exam, Agnes just sat staring at the paper, chewing on her pencil. Aside from learning how to use a library and take fifteen-minute catnaps, the one lesson she learned in college—to memorize information quickly and visually—was perhaps the most important tool Agnes would later bring to her career as a dancer and choreographer.

Though Agnes enjoyed the freedom from the rigors of dance in her freshman year, it wasn't long before she found herself slowly being drawn back. On one occasion, she volunteered to dance for a benefit to raise money for students who were victims of a campus fire. Her performance brought offers to join three sororities; Agnes finally settled on the Beta Xi chapter of Kappa Alpha Theta. Despite all the years of dance lessons and countless hours of practice, the benefit was the first time Agnes had ever stepped onto a stage. After that event, she agreed to stage occasional dances for student rallies, enlisting the help of her sorority sisters.

Dr. Campbell, dismayed by Agnes's dance activities, reminded her that she didn't have the graceful body necessary to make a serious career as a dancer. She preferred that Agnes write, but she advised her talented young student that, if she just *had* to be onstage, she should pursue a career as a tragic actress. After all, Agnes had grown up around the discipline, visiting her uncle Cecil's movie sets, watching some of the best actors and actresses of the silent-movie era. From them she learned how to use gestures and pantomime to express a character's emotions. As an adolescent Agnes had pored over photos and text in books on period costumes and set design. Her dancing may still have been a bit amateurish, but her costume designs were very realistic and, thanks to Anna's teaching, created and sewn like those of the best studio lot professionals.

In her junior year, Agnes put on a skit at the UCLA Press Club Vodevil. It was a great success; the university's *Morning Club Bulletin* wrote, "Those who have never seen [Agnes] dance will have something to remember when their youth is over." (Easton, 46) For the performance, Agnes wanted to demonstrate how closely related jazz dance was to the jungle. Even Agnes's father attended the performance, and he was noticeably impressed. She continued to put on dance performances, including one set to four sonnets written by the Italian poet Petrarch. For the dances, Agnes dressed the girls to look just like the nymphs in the paintings of Sandro Botticelli. The costumes were a bit risqué, but despite objections from UCLA director Dr. E.C. Moore, Agnes refused to change them.

With dance back in her life, Agnes resumed practicing. She quickly realized that she was quite out of shape. Still without any conscious intention to return to dance as her life's work, she endured the grueling practices and aches and pains that came with a return to fitness.

In her senior year, Agnes met Douglass "Dug" Montgomery, an aspiring stage actor whom Margaret had eyed at the Pasadena Playhouse. Dug seemed more interested in seeing Agnes dance than in dating Margaret. After seeing one of her amateur shows at the Friday Morning Club, Dug was convinced that Agnes was no amateur.

Soon Dug and Agnes became kindred spirits—able to talk endlessly about theater, acting, and dance. He often encouraged her to leave school and start a professional career in dance, telling her she was a great performer and had a duty to follow her calling. De Mille wrote of his effect on her resolve: "No trumpets sound when the important decisions of our life are made. Destiny is made known silently. The wheels turn within our hearts for years and suddenly everything meshes and we are lifted into the next level of progress. . . . This boy simply said what I had waited all my life to hear." (De Mille, *Piper*, 77)

Of course, Agnes fell in love with Dug, but her affections were never returned. Dug kept their relationship platonic, but he enjoyed their time together and appreciated their mutual love of the arts. As her college life drew to a close, Agnes

Dug Montgomery. As a senior at UCLA, de Mille met and fell in love with Douglass "Dug" Montgomery, an aspiring actor. Montgomery was captivated by de Mille's spirit and talent, but he did not return her feelings. Still, they became close friends, and he actively encouraged her professional development over the course of their friendship, which lasted for many years.

struggled with many doubts about a future in dance. At nineteen, she was as old as Pavlova had been when she'd made her professional dance debut. Exams had mentally exhausted and drained Agnes. She was out of shape and wondered if she could even get her body back into the condition necessary to pursue dance.

With these nagging questions hanging in the air, Agnes graduated from UCLA cum laude, all the while really yearning to dance as Pavlova had in *La Sylphide* but believing in her heart that she'd never be that good. If accepting the limitations of her future didn't make her heart heavy enough, her parents' news the next day surely did: Anna and William were divorcing. As Carol Easton writes in *No Intermissions*, "The divorce was a cataclysmic end to Agnes's charmed childhood. . . . Real life, for which she was almost totally unprepared, had begun." (49)

5

No One Dances in America

1927–1932

"We are interested in you," my theater friends used to say, "because you are more than a dancer. You are an actress." But I knew one could not be more than a dancer—being an actress was less.

—Agnes de Mille, *Dance to the Piper*

Agnes took the news of her parents' divorce hard, but it was even harder for Anna to reconcile the breakup. There was another woman in William's life, one he would eventually marry. Anna, on the other hand, turned to her daughters for comfort and companionship. The three de Mille women went to Europe for what remained of the summer and then, instead of returning to Hollywood, took up residence once again in New York City.

William provided generous financial support for Anna and his daughters, and he gave Anna the cottage at Merriewold as

De Mille onstage, c. 1930. Meeting obstacle after obstacle in her quest to achieve greatness in the art of dance, de Mille turned her attention toward choreography. Working in choreography involved weaving together her talents of storytelling, characterization, theatrics, and movement, expanding the experience of dance and its place in the context of theater. Her early works combined her talents as dancer and choreographer, for she performed them herself.

part of the divorce settlement. Anna leased a large duplex apartment, and they all pooled their income to pay the high cost of food and rent in the city. Still exhausted from college, Agnes took some time to take stock of her talents and skills, wanting to be certain that despite all the reasons why entering a career in dance was not advisable, she should forge ahead. Intellectually, she knew it was not a good move, but her heart allowed no room for any other option.

Before de Mille left for Europe, Dug told her that he was heading for New York, where live stage performance still thrived, and advised her to do the same. He'd found work in a stage production almost as soon as he arrived, and he was doing well. Dug learned the professional etiquette of an up-and-coming performer in the business—dressing better and making sure he knew the names of all the managers and agents in town, where to dine, and even what cocktail parties to attend. He urged de Mille to change her name, dye her hair, have her nose fixed, and have her teeth straightened. She refused, determined to maintain herself as she was, successful or not.

The de Mille family name would not be an asset in Agnes's quest to succeed in theater. There were few opportunities to dance in America. Determined to start somewhere, de Mille continued to take dance classes and, at Dug's suggestion, began to put together pieces for a dance concert. She rented a recital hall and hired a pianist. Dug helped her enhance her acting skills, showing her how every gesture, every movement, conveyed some form of expression. Wrote de Mille, "He taught me to establish with a single gesture the atmosphere and inner rhythm of a personality. He forced me to establish mood with posture." (De Mille, *Piper*, 85)

Instead of creating dances that simply moved to the music, de Mille crafted character studies using dance as a natural part of the event in which the personality of the individual is revealed. Since de Mille felt she was stronger at pantomime and acting than dance, the acted story seemed the logical approach when constructing her works. De Mille acknowledged that she was not really creating "dances;" they were more like character studies where dance was the adornment, infused with traditional folk or theatrical steps. De Mille used dance steps in much the same way as the costumes, lighting, and music included in the theatrical show—to create the illusion and set the stage and mood for a performance.

De Mille drew from her own background and experience in creating her dances. Her first, entitled '49, told the story of a young pioneer girl traveling west with others during the California Gold Rush of 1848–1849. She believed it was the first dance created that showcased American folk-style material, including a version of a square dance.

She based other early studies on the paintings and sculptures she had seen by the French artist Edgar Degas. The idea for *Stage Fright* (1927) came to de Mille after she saw a Degas statuette of a young ballerina at the Metropolitan Museum of Art. The sculpture depicted not the glamour of the ballet star, but rather the unglamorous part—the toil and pain a dancer experiences from hours of practice.

De Mille created *Stage Fright* to share with the audience what it's like behind the scenes as a dancer. De Mille chose to play a terrified dancer doing warm-ups at the barre and performing other backstage rituals, such as practicing moves and sprinkling water on the floor before starting her exercises to prevent skidding. To anyone's knowledge, this was the first time something like this had ever been done. As Carol Easton explained in *No Intermissions*, for Agnes de Mille, *Stage Fright* was important for more than its entertainment value alone:

> [*Stage Fright*] demonstrated her extraordinary ability to
> convey, without words, her thoughts and feelings to the

audience. She saw the humor in the situation—couldn't *not* see it—but saw its life-or-death seriousness, as well. By making tragedy funny and comedy sad, she brought tears to the eyes of the laughing audience. (56)

De Mille worked to create a series of such pieces in preparation for her anticipated debut on the New York stage.

AUDITIONING AND PERFORMING

When de Mille felt she had enough of a repertoire, she began auditioning for agents, whom she sardonically called "The Boys" and described as resembling "newspaper reporters at an inquest." (De Mille, *Piper*, 87) Most were not writers, directors, set designers, or producers, nor were they perceptive of talent. What they could do was sense what was commercial (having broad appeal), and they had connections to most of the producers outside of Hollywood. De Mille auditioned and auditioned, certain that over a period of time she had danced in front of every known manager and agent in the business in New York.

When de Mille had no success in breaking into commercial theater, her mother suggested that she stage a concert performance in Santa Fe, New Mexico, where her friend Mary Hunter and aunt Mary Austin could help promote the concert and gather other friends to attend. They set out for Santa Fe, where Anna searched for a theater and Agnes a pianist. Tickets were printed, announcements were sent, and it all came together quite nicely one warm summer evening.

The next day *The Santa Fe New Mexican* reported of de Mille's performance, "Her natural grace, her exquisite facial expression, her accomplished technique developed through years of training under a famous Russian master, will undoubtedly make her known soon as one of the great dancers of America." (Easton, 58) Anna, pleased with the reception her daughter's work received, was also pleased with the evening's take—$364—which covered expenses.

When de Mille returned to New York, she continued to look for jobs. In January 1928, she agreed to split the cost of putting on a concert at the Republic Theater with dancer Jacques Cartier. De Mille's program consisted of seven original pieces, the most well-received being *Stage Fright* and another Degas study called *Ballet Class*. Opening night's performance, to de Mille's astonishment, was in front of a full house. Despite being short on stage presence and experience, de Mille performed as if she had been on a stage most of her life.

The audience loved the show, and so did *New York Times* dance critic John Martin, who wrote, "Here is undoubtedly one of the brightest stars now rising above our native horizon." (De Mille, *Piper*, 94) After seeing another show that included *'49*, Martin wrote that the heart and soul of de Mille's work rested in "her rare and intuitive understanding of human beings" and that she shared Charlie Chaplin's ability to view tragedy through the perspective of comedy. Even though the three shows Cartier and de Mille put on did well at the box office, there wasn't any money to go further. Since no managers or agents had attended any of the performances, no new opportunities arose.

De Mille continued to work on creating new dances and auditioning. When she heard that London talent manager Charles Cochran and playwright Noel Coward were casting a new revue, de Mille arranged to audition for them. Though they were courteous, both men felt de Mille was better suited to the concert hall than the stage. Later that afternoon, as Agnes sat at home dejected, Anna offered her encouragement by sharing consoling words from Henry George: "My father used to say, that a way would become apparent as we go along. In the end a door always opens." (De Mille, *Piper*, 95)

PROFESSIONAL BREAKTHROUGHS

After working all summer on new dances, de Mille did land a two-week engagement at the Roxy Theater. Finally, her first break came through a friend—Ruth Page, a Chicago-based dancer and choreographer whom she had met through Ruth St. Denis. De Mille appeared with Page in a program in Ravinia, Illinois; while there, Page introduced de Mille to a member of Diaghilev's company, the Russian

EDGAR DEGAS

The art of the nineteenth-century French painter and sculptor Edgar Degas reveals the passion with which he explored color, composition, and form. His style has greatly influenced contemporary art. It was his studies on canvas and his sculptures of ballet dancers that inspired some of Agnes de Mille's early dances, including *Stage Fright* (1927).

The son of a wealthy Franco-Italian banking family, Hilaire-Germain Edgar Degas was free to pursue his artistic talent without the burden of making a living. With his family's encouragement and financial security, Degas never had to be concerned with pleasing art critics or the public. Having so few constraints permitted him to create his art on his own terms, with only the pressures he imposed on himself.

Degas was particularly fascinated with creating works in which the artist was an unseen observer. Fascinated by the details of everyday life, he painted scenes as if he were observing his subjects through a keyhole. He captured elements of the world whose meaning other painters of his time had not yet come to understand—a cast-off dress that maintains its wearer's form; a ballet student who scratches her back while listening to her instructor; a laundress who yawns while doing her work. He dancer Adolph Bolm. Bolm had put together a small dance company of his own called Ballet Intime, which included fifteen members and a small orchestra conducted by Louis Horst. De Mille was invited to replace Page and dance three of her solo pieces while Ballet Intime was on a six-week fall tour.

The tour was a good experience for de Mille, and the income was very much needed. Having a paying engagement

was among the first artists to pursue the "backstage" aspects of life; in fact, he is known for his candid depictions of ballet dancers in their off-guard moments—stretching, tying their shoes. (This perspective seized de Mille's imagination when she saw Degas's sculptural studies of dancers. She began to think of showing the audience the stresses of ballet practice and the pre-performance rituals of the dancer.)

Degas's work sought to find the line that rendered life precisely, with the goal of creating a representation that captured the living, breathing individual. His studies of nudes were done realistically. He did not idealize his subjects or "beautify" them in any way; if a woman he was painting was heavy or had visible bumps and indents in her skin, he painted those traits. His nudes were therefore not always flattering. When asked why he painted some of his women so ugly, Degas replied that, in general, women *were* ugly.

Despite his looking at the outside world to find models and situations to create his art, Edgar Degas was a rather shy, insecure, and aloof young man. He had few friends, preferring to live reclusively, painting and creating sculptures instead of interacting with the life beyond the walls of his studio.

was a welcome change for de Mille, who often wondered how long she'd have to live off of Anna's money. Working with Adolph Bolm was special for de Mille, too. He had danced with her idol, Anna Pavlova, and was a talented dancer in his own right. He was not a good manager, though, and this tour would be the company's last.

Though Ballet Intime did not survive, de Mille found a valuable friend in conductor Louis Horst. Over the years, Horst had helped many people in the dance world, including Martha Graham, Doris Humphrey, Ruth St. Denis, and Ted Shawn. He had taught and composed music for almost every concert dancer in the industry. De Mille believed that, over the years, Horst "influenced and helped the dancing in this country more than any other non-dancer." (De Mille, *Piper*, 99) Horst loved Martha Graham and talked about her often. He told de Mille that he wanted her to see Graham perform when they returned to New York. Instead, de Mille went to see Antonia Mercé, called "La Argentina." Her dancing took de Mille's breath away.

In a way, seeing La Argentina's show was a kind of vindication for de Mille. La Argentina danced solo the whole evening, accompanied only by a pianist. Every detail of her program was professionally presented, from the costuming to the music to the energetic movements in her dances. She was beautiful, and there was a magnetism about her that seemed to draw people into her, wholly and completely. La Argentina, in de Mille's eyes, was supreme, from her terrific sense of rhythm—arms, feet, castanets, and swinging skirt all in sync with the music—to her sense of composition, her very womanly presence, and her bewitching smile.

De Mille desperately wanted to create her own show, but launching one would cost thousands of dollars. She knew the facts—in the late 1920s and early 1930s a single concert performance cost about $1,200, and that did not include the rehearsals and costumes. At that time, Martha Graham

Adolph Bolm and Thamar Karsavina in *Firebird*, 1911.
Through a friend, de Mille met the Russian dancer Adolph Bolm,
formerly of St. Petersburg's Maryinsky Ballet and then of Sergey
Diaghilev's company. This introduction lead to de Mille's being
invited to replace a principal dancer in Bolm's own small
dance company, Ballet Intime. On a six-week fall tour with the
company, de Mille danced three solo pieces, working for an
income that was modest but needed. Perhaps the most important
benefits of this time for de Mille were the opportunity to work
with Bolm, who had danced with the great Pavlova, and the
connection she developed with the company's conductor, Louis
Horst. This is one of several photographs of *Firebird* published by
E.O. Hoppé, one of the nineteenth century's great photographers.

was the only dancer who could earn more than $1,200—few other dancers were even able to stage a recital. Anna was funding Agnes's recitals and losing quite a lot of money.

Just when it looked bleakest for de Mille's career, she was offered a job choreographing and dancing in a revival of Christopher Morley's musical melodrama *The Black Crook*. *The Black Crook* had been staged many times all over North America since its original appearance in 1866. This 1929 revival was going to be staged across the river in Hoboken, New Jersey. It was the first time that de Mille was being given the opportunity to choreograph for a group. Working with a partner seemed like a good idea, and de Mille also needed a *dance* partner, for she was to perform in the show. The dance critic John Martin, now a friend of de Mille's, sent Leonard Warren to audition for de Mille.

Not only could Warren dance, he could act—and de Mille brought him on as a collaborator. He had an edge to his personality, though, often telling de Mille she wasn't disciplined enough, she was too fat, too slow, that she didn't have enough energy to be a dancer. He relentlessly pushed her to the limit during their four-hour-long rehearsals. He disagreed with de Mille about music choices, corrected her grammar, and criticized her clothing. Warren was abruptly shaking de Mille into the harsh realities of the dance world. He was just as hard on himself as he was on de Mille, but that was small consolation.

On opening night, the whole production was in disarray. The performance lasted five and a half hours. Still, Martin wrote a splendid review. During another performance, Warren accidentally kicked de Mille in the face, breaking her nose. Neither of them skipped a beat, and de Mille assured Warren that it wasn't his fault. The break did not do much to help the shape of her nose, though, and de Mille continued to perform with splints up her nostrils.

She soon became fatigued and fed up with doing the

same thing every night in front of a rowdy audience "tanked up" on beer and constantly munching snacks while she danced. When her three-month commitment was up in June, de Mille went back to auditioning.

FROM THE PINNACLE TO THE PITS

William had kept in touch with his daughters by letter, though he had not seen or spoken to Agnes since the divorce. After waiting an acceptable amount of time, William had married screenwriter Clara Beranger, and he wanted his daughters to acknowledge her as his wife. In 1930, William wrote to Agnes and offered to pay her train fare to come to California for a visit. He enticed her with the news that he had arranged with the studio a screen test, in which she could perform a few of her dances. Perhaps working in sound movies would provide the break she was looking for in her stalled career.

With little happening in her life in New York, Agnes accepted William's invitation. She arrived in Los Angeles in June with Anna, Margaret, and Leonard in tow. With Anna's money and Leonard's accompaniment, de Mille intended to put on her own dance concert. It was a true homecoming for de Mille, though she refused to take advantage of the family for any assistance, creature comforts or otherwise. She was going to do this on her own (with Anna's money, of course), without exploiting her famous last name to court special favors.

De Mille rented the Music Box Theater, found a stage manager, and hired a press agent—Agnes O'Malley, who also represented Oscar Hammerstein II. De Mille worked for eight days to prepare the show. She refused to see anyone during that time, including William, except for college professor Lily Campbell. De Mille rehearsed her dances until they were perfect. Once she was confident about her performance she was no longer nervous, even though she'd

Leonard Warren in *Il Trovatore*, 1955. De Mille met Warren in 1929, when she brought him on for *The Black Crook*; the two collaborated again on the disastrous *Flying Colors* and remained close. Warren was hard on de Mille as a dancer, but he told her what she needed to hear. He went on to become an accomplished baritone with the Metropolitan Opera; here he is shown in costume as the Conte di Luna in Verdi's opera *Il Trovatore*.

be playing in front of a sold-out audience that included William and Clara, other family members, friends, old schoolmates, childhood friends, and former teachers.

If she was going to make it in dance, de Mille couldn't have picked a more discerning audience with which to test the waters. Granted, these people had a personal connection in her life, but de Mille also wanted to show the world that she was talented and that she had the stuff to achieve her own piece of success. Anna was unfailing in support of her daughter, but William was quite another matter. He had been adamantly opposed to his daughter's dancing and had attended only one or two amateur recitals. Only now, after years of resistance, was he suddenly supportive.

De Mille decided to open the performance with *Stage Fright*. When the curtain went up, she came out swinging the watering can to sprinkle the floor. The audience responded with an approving laugh. De Mille danced splendidly, feeling that she had never danced better in her life. It was the realization of a dream. The next day, the newspapers trumpeted her success with flattering reviews. *Stage* wrote, "Agnes de Mille instantly captured her house—not as a friend, or as anybody's daughter or granddaughter, but as a great artist in her own right. . . . She's a story teller, an illustrator, a poet, caricaturist, portraitist, dramatist, pantomimist, comedian, satirist, humorist, designer, and dancer. . . . Most terpsichorean performers dance with their feet; she danced with her head." (Easton, 82)

After the performance, Agnes O'Malley brought Hammerstein backstage to introduce him to de Mille. He told her that he thought her pieces showed obvious talent but wasn't sure how it could be best utilized. Twelve years later, while Hammerstein was preparing *Oklahoma!*, de Mille went to see him to suggest such a way. The after-show festivities continued with a party, graciously thrown by Uncle Cecil. De Mille was sure that she would get a job now.

Enthusiastic about his niece's concert, Cecil offered to finance a road show, but the timeframe he had in mind — to be ready to go on tour in two months — was unrealistic. Since it had taken de Mille three years to create six good dances, she told him she could be ready in two years. Cecil told her it was a now-or-never offer. When de Mille suggested that he offer her a job, Cecil rejected the idea. After all, she was family. After her rather uninspired response to his offer, he once again saw de Mille as a dowdy, insecure girl not likely to make it in show business.

When de Mille finally saw her father, he was of no help, either. He really knew nothing about the concert business and offered little advice on how to build on the success of her show. Dejected, de Mille returned to New York. She decided to move out of her mother's apartment and get her own place. By now, Margaret had married. At twenty-five, de Mille wanted to see if she could make it on her own. With her allowance from William, she rented a small inside suite in a deteriorating uptown hotel and got back to work, though it seemed as if she were spinning her wheels.

Warren was becoming desperate for work, too, and he didn't have a monthly allowance to fall back on. Before giving up totally — de Mille had faced that moment so many times already — de Mille and Warren gathered a small group of dancers and prepared one last audition. This one was for a Broadway show called *Flying Colors*. The three men involved in the project were all heavyweights in musical theater — lyricist Howard Dietz, composer Arthur Schwartz, and producer Max Gordon.

After a small conference following their audition, Gordon offered the choreography job to de Mille and Warren. It was a catastrophe waiting to happen. Never having choreographed anything but *The Black Crook*, de Mille and Warren had little experience, and definitely no experience with a large troupe or with the management of an entire show. Dietz and Schwartz

Rehearsal for Albertina Rasch's *Wild Violets*, London, September 1932. *Flying Colors* was a crushing failure for de Mille, who lacked the self-confidence to realize her vision. She and Leonard Warren were encouraged to leave the production, and she recommended the choreographer Albertina Rasch as her replacement. Rasch, a former student of the Royal Opera Ballet School in Vienna, had been dancing and choreographing on Broadway since 1911. Her troupe, the Albertina Rasch Girls, danced with the Ziegfeld Follies, toured the world, and even danced at the Moulin Rouge in Paris.

selected the dancers on looks rather than ability. Costumes were chosen without any regard for how the dancers were going to move in them. The stars of the show, Clifton Webb and Tamara Geva, were given too much freedom in decisions about the dancers. De Mille quickly realized that she was probably the most ill-suited person for the show.

Though she tried to muddle her way through rehearsals, it was clear that nothing was coming together. When Geva rehearsed, she seemed to take over. A timid de Mille couldn't find the nerve to tell her to leave. In *Dance to the Piper*, de Mille sadly explained her lack of confidence at the time:

> I had not the gall to tell her to leave, nor the courage to continue. . . . It took me more than a decade of effort before I could say "Clear the hall." Had I had the guts then to say what comes so easily years later, my story might have been happier. I wish the girl of 1932, drawn, white and quivering and sweating cold, could see me ready the decks for action now. (128)

As time went on with no improvement either in de Mille's control or command of the job or in the cast's cooperation, she actually began to pray that the taxi she took to the theater would wind up in an accident, if only to postpone the day's torture for just a little while. Slowly but surely, de Mille and Warren were being pushed out of their involvement in the show.

By opening night in Philadelphia, one dreary night in September, de Mille and Warren knew the show was lost. Dance numbers didn't work, the audience seemed confused about what they were watching, and there was no continuity to the show.

The next morning, Dietz summoned de Mille to his office. He got straight to the point, telling de Mille that five new dance numbers needed to be created in five days. De Mille told him she couldn't do it. She was too exhausted from the whole experience and didn't want to have to pull the cooperation from the dancers. It was a deeply painful moment for her. To salvage the show, de Mille suggested that Dietz hire choreographer Albertina Rasch, telling him that she was among the best.

De Mille and Warren packed up their belongings and drove back to New York. During the silent ride home, de Mille reviewed her past, trying to come to terms with this ultimate failure. She thought about her choices in life, her relationship with her mother and father, her inability to say no when saying yes avoided a confrontation. Then she turned her attention to the future. With the country in the grips of an economic depression, with few dance opportunities in the United States, and after the total debacle of *Flying Colors*, she wondered yet again whether there were a future in dance.

6

Crisscrossing the Atlantic

1932–1934

The universe lies before you on the floor, in the air, in the mysterious bodies of your dancers, in your mind. From this voyage no one returns poor or weary.

—Agnes de Mille, *To a Young Dancer*

With the disaster of *Flying Colors* still very fresh and painful in her mind, de Mille was torn between her stubborn determination to follow a career in dance against her father's wishes and how incredible she felt when she stepped on a stage and let dancing melt away all her worries and insecurities. During her musing, she remembered a conversation she'd had with Antonia Mercé, known as La Argentina, the year before. La Argentina had told de Mille that she believed rhythm was the common denominator of American and Spanish dancing. As she had found and developed the

Dame Marie Rambert, 1925. Like many artists, Rambert was described as someone capable of great sweetness but also of driving a person mad. Demanding as she may have been, though, she was known for developing students of prominence in dance. Madame Rambert recognized de Mille's talent and offered her the opportunity to study and perform at the Mercury Theatre in London. De Mille enjoyed the taste of independence of this time in her life and the chance to interact with colleagues in the field of her creative passion.

Spanish rhythm, so too must de Mille find and develop American rhythm.

In the fall of 1932, La Argentina's manager, Arnold Meckel, urged de Mille to let him sponsor her in Paris concerts, where the cost was much less than in New York. Having nothing to lose, de Mille thought she and Leonard Warren should try to launch a career abroad. Anna financed the trip, except for $1,000 that de Mille borrowed from her new brother-in-law, Bernard Fineman. In October, the three boarded the *Île de France* and sailed for Europe.

De Mille danced in Paris, Brussels, and London. There were problems in the first two cities on the tour, however. Meckel had not arranged things or promoted de Mille's appearances in Paris and Brussels as promised, and Anna had to ensure that her daughter danced in acceptable theaters in front of good-sized audiences. De Mille's performances received a lukewarm reception in Paris and Brussels, perhaps because the audiences didn't understand her pieces. Whatever the reason, de Mille was happy to move on to London.

With the assistance of actor, director, and longtime family friend Romney Brent, de Mille's time in London was much more pleasant. Brent escorted de Mille all around London, taking her to meet friends including Raymond Massey, Noel Coward, and Dame May Whitty. When introducing de Mille, Brent declared she was "the greatest pantomimic artist in the world." (De Mille, *Piper*, 140) They all came to see de Mille dance at the Arts Theatre Club. In fact, she performed in front of a sold-out house.

MARIE RAMBERT AND THE MERCURY THEATRE

Not long after her London performances, de Mille benefited from an important introduction to playwright Ashley Dukes and his wife, dancer Marie Rambert. A tempestuous woman, the Polish-born Rambert had a complex personality—

she could be warm, insightful, and caring, but she also had uncontrollable outbursts, sometimes over the smallest problems. She operated one of the few ballet companies and dance schools in England and was known to have an almost infallible eye for talent. She boldly said to de Mille, "I can teach you much. Stay and study with me." (De Mille, *Piper*, 140) As an added incentive to stay, Dukes and Rambert invited de Mille to give a series of concert performances at their Mercury Theatre.

The opportunity to dance regularly and study with Rambert appealed to de Mille, even though a large chunk of the money she'd earn from her recitals would end up paying for her lessons. For the first time in her life, though, de Mille had a chance to be on her own, in a creative environment surrounded by colleagues striving toward similar goals.

Anna and Leonard Warren went back to New York, and de Mille got a room at the English-Speaking Union near Berkeley Square. By de Mille family standards, the accommodations were meager. The room had few furnishings and was rather small, but in de Mille's eyes, it was quiet and cozy. She was quite happy and looked forward to the possibilities that lay ahead.

Rambert's Ballet Club and Dukes's Mercury Theatre coexisted in the same building, which at one time had been the vestry house of an oddly shaped church. The exterior looked like what it had been, but the inside was a multilevel maze carved up by hallways, small closets, stairwells, and a small auditorium. The Ballet Club became the site of the renaissance of English dance. It is where Frederick Aston made his way in dance, where Antony Tudor developed into one of the finest choreographers Europe had ever seen, and where Alicia Markova got to perform regularly at a time when most places wouldn't give her the chance.

Many important dancers had pirouetted across Rambert's

practice hall and into prominence in the industry. They all studied and worked for Madame Rambert. Without question, Rambert did a lot for English dance, but when asked, people always gave her mixed reviews. Some would lose all control at the mention of her name. Her name sometimes brought tears to eyes, or drained blood from a face. She could drive people crazy, but most agreed that Marie Rambert could also be very sweet. With the right people attending to the business of the organization, Rambert might have succeeded in guiding the Ballet Club and Mercury Theatre into national prominence.

It was in this company that de Mille met Antony Tudor and Hugh Laing. Both men would eventually come to the United States and earn great recognition for their work in dance and choreography. Tudor, who was Rambert's "everything man"—secretary of the school, stage manager, accompanist, and handyman—occasionally pitched in to handle lighting and curtain operation when de Mille gave a recital. In a brief time, de Mille, Tudor, and Laing became not only colleagues, but friends. The two men often accompanied de Mille on shopping excursions and exploratory trips through London's street markets and outlying counties.

A year after meeting "the boys," de Mille asked Laing to partner with her in a concert she was giving at the Mercury Theatre. He was a natural actor, and his dramatic dance style was a wonderful complement to de Mille's own style. Tudor, besides dancing, was developing his choreographic skills, and in 1934, he created *Jardin aux Lilas*.

It was clear that all three of them were coming into their own as artists. Though it was a joyous time to be in London—pleasant weather had descended upon the British city, blue skies and flowers filled the landscape with color, and a few ballet companies came through, filling evening after evening with breathtaking performances—

de Mille, Tudor, and Laing were also working very hard developing and honing their talents. De Mille took a lesson every day, sometimes with Tudor. It was Tudor who helped de Mille understand the principles behind the technique in dance.

For the next several years, de Mille traveled back and forth between England and the United States. During that time, she developed a following of admirers who enjoyed her dance themes honoring American culture and delighted in her style and humor. De Mille became a serious student of dance, reading all she could about its history, as well as being an astute observer of human and animal movements. When creating a dance, de Mille wanted the steps and moves to be accurate representations.

FRIENDS IN NEED

During her time alone in England, de Mille wrote detailed letters to Anna about her days. She was the granddaughter of Henry George, so there were plenty of English "Georgists" to fill de Mille's social time. She also had little difficulty mixing with the artistic and political elite.

One of the people de Mille befriended at that time, however, had no connection to her English circle of friends and acquaintances. A former classmate of de Mille's had written a few introductory letters on her behalf to people he had known while at Oxford University. One of them was a paralyzed young man named Ramon Reed. The introductory letter led to a mutually enjoyable friendship that lasted from their first meeting in May 1933 until Reed's death three years later.

De Mille and Reed were wonderful companions. He held a special place in de Mille's heart. Ramon was well-read, charming, bright, and an unending supporter of her work. He constantly offered words of encouragement, never wavering in his faith in her talent, even during the most

(Continued on page 90)

MARIE RAMBERT AND A BRIEF HISTORY OF BALLET

The earliest form of ballet dates to Italy during the Renaissance—specifically, the fifteenth century. Elaborate forms of entertainment, known as court ballets, were performed in large chambers usually used for banquets and balls. The court ballets incorporated many art forms, including painting, poetry, music, and dancing. They were staged between banquet courses and were often related to the menu; for example, the story of Jason and the Golden Fleece might precede a course of roast lamb.

The Italian court ballets were further developed in France. Ballets consisted of elaborate costumes and set designs with choreography that accentuated floor patterns, since audiences saw most performances from above. By the eighteenth century, dance had evolved into an opera-ballet style, where singing and dancing were linked by a common theme. Advances in ballet dance technique (pirouettes, leaps, and jumps) began with the introduction of dramatic ballet, presentations that emphasized action through dance, with fewer spoken elements.

In 1832, the first Romantic ballet, *La Sylphide*, introduced a new style of dance, one in which the human and supernatural worlds were differentiated.

While an imbalance in female and male dancers led to a decline in ballet in France, the Russians managed to preserve and further develop the art. The choreographer Marius Petipa perfected the full-length, evening-long production. *The Sleeping Beauty* (1890) and *Swan Lake* (1895) were set to the musical scores of the famed Russian composer Pyotr Ilich Tchaikovsky. When the Russian impresario Sergey Diaghilev founded his Ballets Russes at the beginning of the twentieth century, the choreographer Michel Fokine worked to create ballets that were even more expressive and authentic, both in staging and in costuming. The company presented a wide range of productions that included scores from classical composers, including *The Firebird*, *Scheherazade*, and *Petrushka*. The Ballets Russes also introduced the world to ballet greats Vaslav Nijinsky and Anna Pavlova.

Ballet companies similar to the Ballets Russes began emerging all over the world as Pavlova, Fokine, and others formed their own companies and worked with those who were establishing others. One former member of the Ballets Russes was the Polish-born dancer Dame Marie Rambert, who also was a founder of British ballet. Rambert was married to the playwright Ashley Dukes. In 1926, she established the Ballet Club, a school and dance company, and Dukes created the Mercury Theatre to present dance and drama performances.

Many of the great stars of dance and choreography in the 1930s and 1940s began their careers with Rambert at the Ballet Club. In addition to Agnes de Mille, Rambert's group included the choreography greats Antony Tudor and Frederick Ashton, as well as the dancers Hugh Laing, Diana Gould, Pearl Argyle, and William Chappell.

The Ballet Club opened on February 16, 1931. By the end of 1932, the Ballet Club, later renamed the Marie Rambert Dancers, had more than 1,700 members, and it had become fashionable to attend the group's Sunday night performances. The Rambert Dance Company is the oldest active dance company in Great Britain and employs more artists than any other contemporary dance company in the United Kingdom.

Marie Rambert died in 1982 after suffering a stroke. During her lifetime, she earned much respect from colleagues and many honors, including *chevalier, Légion d'Honneur* (1957) and Dame Commander of the British Empire (1962).

(Continued from page 87)

difficult moments. De Mille became one of Reed's lifelines to the outside world, bringing people from all professions—writers, actors, musicians, and even some of the Single Taxers—to his home. She also managed to get him to leave his otherwise cocooned world, arranging for him to come to her performances, scheduling afternoon tea or a picnic outside, or planning a trip to the cinema.

De Mille got her first paying job in England through the helping hand of Romney Brent. She was hired to create the dances for *Nymph Errant*, a musical that was produced by Charles Cochran and that starred English actress and dancer Gertrude Lawrence. Cole Porter wrote the music and lyrics for the show, and Brent signed on as director.

The opening night in Manchester, the tryout city for the show, was a dazzling event for de Mille. She arrived by taxi with Brent and friends Noel Coward and Douglas Fairbanks, Jr. For the first time, de Mille's name was listed in a performance program alone, credited beneath "Dances and Ensembles by."

De Mille's dances in *Nymph Errant* were well-received by an audience packed with celebrities, but the press was less receptive. Before the company was ready for its London premiere, de Mille was asked to create a new dance and make changes in another. Feeling suddenly insecure, she recalled the failure of *Flying Colors*. A health crisis with Reed gave de Mille an escape from the pressure, and she stayed with him until the crisis passed. When she returned to Manchester, de Mille was told that Cochran had brought in someone else to rework the dances in question. It was not quite the humiliation of *Flying Colors*, though; her dances remained in the show and her name was left in the program.

Deeply confused, de Mille wondered how her work could begin well only to deteriorate, and how promises of being promoted always seemed to fade once the initial enthusiasm passed, or the theater halls booked turned out to be places in desperate need of renovation. Some of those who offered to help also seemed to take advantage financially, not being forthright about gate receipts. She had been compared to Charlie Chaplin, she had dance hits on the London circuit, and yet de Mille was unable to jump-start her career financially, creatively, or in salability. She felt as if she took one step forward only to falter and fall two steps back.

Once again, it was one of de Mille's friends who offered her work. Romney Brent hired de Mille to create two ballets for a new show he was going to direct called *Why Not Tonight?* The first piece called for a dancer to represent the wind amid a garden of flowers. The other, written by Reed, was entitled *Three Virgins and a Devil.* A light comedy, the story depicted a new devil tempting three virgins to follow him into hell. De Mille cast Tudor, Laing, and some of the students from Rambert's Ballet Club.

Once again, fate intervened, leaving de Mille barely two weeks to prepare. This time it was because one of her prayers had been answered. Uncle Cecil had cabled his niece to come to Hollywood to create a dance for his film project *Cleopatra.*

Though Reed always knew that de Mille's personal life and work might take her home, even perhaps with little notice, he was apprehensive about de Mille's leaving before the revue opening. He would also miss his close friend and companion. Maybe if he had known that the job in California would be a terribly painful and crushing experience for de Mille, he might have tried to keep her from going. De Mille could barely contain her excitement that the call had finally come from Cecil B. de Mille, the great Hollywood film producer.

De Mille left ten days before *Why Not Tonight?* opened in Manchester, turning over the project to the capable

Romney Brent directing, 1954. De Mille's first paying job in England came from her family friend Romney Brent. He asked her to choreograph *Nymph Errant*, a musical starring the English actress and dancer Gertrude Lawrence and featuring the music and lyrics of Cole Porter. At the eleventh hour, de Mille was asked to rework certain numbers; she escaped to be with Ramon Reed, leaving the work to be done without her. Still, Brent hired de Mille again, later in her career. This picture shows Brent (far right) directing actors Tom Helmore and Constance Ford in *One Eye Closed*.

hands of Tudor. Filled with renewed hope about her career, and confident that she could not have left *Why Not Tonight?* in better hands, de Mille departed by train from Paddington Station. As she boarded, she posed for a promotional photo for Paramount photographers, then waved and shouted to those who had come to see her off, "Good-bye. I'm off to dance with a crocodile." (De Mille, *Speak to Me*, 250) She couldn't have known how close she was to the truth.

Breakthrough with an American Ballet

1934–1942

To make up a dance, I still need, as I needed then, a pot of tea, walking space, privacy and an idea. . . . It takes hours daily of blind instinctive moving and fumbling to find the revealing gesture, and the process goes on for weeks before I am ready to start composing. Nor can I think any of this out sitting down. My body does it for me. It happens.

—Agnes de Mille

De Mille's enthusiasm over a chance to work with her uncle was quickly dashed during their first discussion about his vision of the dance pieces. Cecil was impressed by Agnes's *Ouled Naïls* dance, in which she pantomimed as a belly-dancing Algerian prostitute working the local cafés and outdoor courtyards to earn money. Cecil wanted something as striking and seductive for his sultry queen to perform when arousing her tired but savvy Marc Antony. Agnes was to create one

Agnes, Cecil B., and Katherine de Mille on the set of
Cleopatra, 1934. The opportunity to choreograph her
uncle's production of *Cleopatra* was indeed a dream come
true for Agnes—but it turned into more of a nightmare.
Her creative vision differed significantly from her uncle's.
She held her ground, believing her uncle would eventually
agree with her way of thinking; instead, Cecil B. de Mille
rejected his niece's dances and cut the scenes in which
she appeared as a dancer. Agnes left the production sour
on her experience with Hollywood. Pictured with Agnes
and Cecil B. de Mille is Katherine (far right), Cecil's
adopted daughter, who at the time was making *Belle
of the Nineties* with Mae West.

piece that she would dance herself and to oversee a dance sequence aboard Cleopatra's barge.

For the barge scene, Cecil described what he saw as follows: "a net dragged over the side of the ship dripping with water and seaweed and dragged by slaves before the table and couch of Cleopatra and [Marc] Antony, and then the net is opened and with the kelp wrapped around them, beautiful girls come to life, their hair still dripping with the sea water, and lay before Antony the clams of the dinner's first course." (Easton, 110–111) Cecil wanted this series of scenes in the film to be "the most seductive, erotic, beautiful, rhythmic, sensuous" ever seen on the big screen.

While Agnes might have been surprised by Cecil's vision for the barge dance, she was appalled by his suggestion for her solo. The solo dance was intended as a vision for the spellbound Antony, in which he would see a beautiful dancer on a bull brought before him. Agnes had known her uncle's reputation in Hollywood as a producer of the grandiose, but she had not anticipated that their visions for the dance sequences would be so vastly different. In typical de Mille family fashion, Agnes dug in, convinced that once Cecil saw the types of dance she envisioned, he would accept her expertise and talent. It was a terrible miscalculation on her part.

Though Cecil had agreed to let Agnes take charge of the dance creations, once he was on the film set, he deferred to LeRoy Prince, Cecil's rather banal but dependable dance director. Prince always agreed with his boss's ideas and understood that Cecil was in charge of every detail of his films. Agnes understood the bottom line but believed she could bring Cecil around to her way of thinking. Perhaps Agnes didn't realize that Cecil probably had offered her the job only as a favor to Anna. It probably never had occurred to him that his offer would become such a big issue. As was inevitable, the pseudo-collaboration between uncle and niece ended with Cecil rejecting the dances and Agnes leaving the motion picture.

BACK TO THE DRAWING BOARD

Within weeks, de Mille was back in London. She spent the month of August relaxing in the Welsh countryside with Reed, which helped her self-esteem. "Reed supplied a strength, a courage, an intellectual and humorous attitude and an acknowledgment of the importance of my work that I felt I must have or cease to exist as a personality. Let any artist try to live for long without recognition, even private, and see how soon the basic nerve fails," de Mille wrote in *Speak to Me, Dance with Me.* (277)

The disastrous experience on the set of *Cleopatra* might have been the best thing to happen in de Mille's struggling career. Rejuvenated by rest and Reed's nurturing, with perhaps even more determination to succeed, in September, de Mille resumed her class and rehearsal schedule and got back to the business of dance with renewed passion.

Others in the dance world were moving forward—Martha Graham was blazing the trail for modern dance in America, and Ted Shawn had formed his own all-male dance company. De Mille put together five new dances, including *Witch Dance, Lazy Dance*, and *Dance of Death*, and scheduled four recitals in November 1934 at the Mercury Theatre, planning to showcase her new dances in London and New York while keeping in the back of her mind thoughts of someday returning triumphant to Hollywood.

Though the performances had their glitches, audiences stood and applauded enthusiastically. It seemed that de Mille's work was gaining mass appeal. On the last night, de Mille wrote her mother that the final recital was "the best I've ever given. . . . I feel alive for the first time in about six years." (Easton, 120)

After the favorable response to her latest dances from audiences and critics in London, de Mille headed back across the Atlantic Ocean to try them out on a New York audience. She looked forward to returning to the United States but decided she would not let it make or break her career. If

America wasn't receptive to her work, she'd go back to Europe, where audiences were appreciative.

What she hadn't counted on was mixed reviews. Her dancing was praised, but by the time she returned to America, dance tastes had moved from the classic ballet technique to a more "modern" style that had become "all the rage." In their reviews, critics wrote that they had liked de Mille's earlier works, like '49, and thought that audiences might find her work even more enjoyable if she incorporated "the American spirit, the American character and American history" into her dances. (Easton, 122)

BACK TO HOLLYWOOD

Hollywood was the next destination in de Mille's American recital trip. She was offered $2,000 for a single night's performance at the Hollywood Bowl. Reed was traveling to the United States and would arrive in time to see the Hollywood Bowl concert. With about thirty dancers to accompany her, de Mille knew that the show would have to be bold, simple, but big enough to translate to the audience from the huge theatrical stage. De Mille hoped that the show would not only be a success but would also prompt new film jobs.

About 18,000 people—almost a full audience—filled the Bowl's outdoor theater. Though de Mille was pleased with the way she danced, technical problems with the lighting limited the audience's view of the program. The critics weren't sympathetic, and de Mille was left to chalk up another disappointing performance. Reed didn't allow de Mille to brood for long, coaxing her to show him around Los Angeles and Hollywood, take him on trips to the beach, introduce him to friends (including poet e.e. Cummings) attend parties, and generally take advantage of the opportunity to relax and vacation.

Before the summer's end, de Mille headed for Steamboat

Springs, Colorado, where she had secured a two-week teaching job at the Perry-Mansfield Summer School of Dance and Drama. While there, she attended a Saturday night hoedown, and the idea for her American ballet *Rodeo* took root. De Mille enjoyed dancing to the music of "Turkey in the Straw" and other square-dance tunes. When the two weeks were up, de Mille discovered that her time teaching had been personally rewarding and a great success.

Reed had been diagnosed with multiple sclerosis and a severe spinal curvature. After doctors examined him in Los Angeles, de Mille learned that his illness would shorten his life, and she wanted him to take in as much as he felt up to. On their way back to Los Angeles, they spent two nights camping out in the desert under the stars and visited Zuni, New Mexico, to see the Native Americans perform a genuine rain dance. Reed had a splendid summer.

In September, de Mille was offered a job to choreograph the dances in director George Cukor's film version of *Romeo and Juliet*. Work on the film, which was being produced by movie mogul Irving Thalberg, wouldn't start until early winter, so de Mille stayed in Los Angeles, sending Reed sailing back to Europe alone.

FRIENDSHIPS END

For four months' work on *Romeo and Juliet*, de Mille earned $8,000—more money than she had ever made before. More importantly, the million-dollar picture offered de Mille everything she had hoped for—a reasonable schedule to create and rehearse the dance components and all the professional resources (an office, secretary, musicians, etc.) to make her job run more smoothly. Perhaps just as important as the job opportunity for de Mille was the feeling that she was a talented, important part of the motion picture's production. For the first time, de Mille dared to think that she might have a breakthrough in her career.

De Mille went to work and completed the dances in just three weeks' time. She felt quite good about her work and her future. If this job went well, surely more film opportunities would come. Cukor attended several of the dance rehearsals without comment. It wasn't until filming began that Thalberg got his first look, and though he complimented de Mille on her efforts, he told her that the pace of the story had to be maintained, even at the expense of the choreography, if necessary.

When de Mille saw the completed film sequences that included the dances, she found that they were merely background activity instead of the action in a scene. In May, a disappointed de Mille, who believed that she had let success slip through her fingers once again, headed back to London to create new dances and to be consoled by her ever-faithful friend Reed.

It was a long, dreadful summer for de Mille. Reed's health was deteriorating, and a rocky love relationship finally ended. De Mille wasn't sure whether she was devastated or relieved. Exhausted emotionally and physically, de Mille tried to regain her strength as the summer days dragged on.

To her surprise, another choreography job surfaced in America. Actor Leslie Howard, who had starred as Romeo in *Romeo and Juliet*, wanted de Mille to choreograph the dances for his Broadway play-within-a-play of *Hamlet*. Though Reed was very sick by the time de Mille needed to leave for the United States in October, he insisted that she go. Offering encouragement, Reed told de Mille, "[D]on't worry about the work—it will be recognized, I know this. And darling, listen to me, dear—get some happiness. There is in you a terrible need." (De Mille, *Speak to Me*, 365) Not long into her *Hamlet* rehearsals back in New York, de Mille received a cable that Reed had passed away peacefully.

The dances for *Hamlet* met much the same fate as the ones for *Romeo and Juliet*. Once again exhausted and mourning the

De Mille with Norma Shearer, 1936. **Agnes de Mille had a much more positive experience with Hollywood when she worked on George Cukor's *Romeo and Juliet* (1936), in which Norma Shearer played Juliet. This work earned de Mille more money than she had ever made before and, more important, enabled her to work in a fully professional capacity with all the resources she needed to do the job well. She was satisfied with her work on the film and began at last to feel the possibility of professional success. De Mille's cousin Katherine appears uncredited in the film as Rosaline, Romeo's initial love interest.**

loss of her friend, de Mille headed back to London. She surrounded herself with the people who had become her tight circle of companions—friends Rebecca West, Elizabeth Bowden, and Reed's cousin Joan; her business manager, Lisa Hewitt; faithful and kind rehearsal pianist Nora Stevenson; and colleagues Tudor and Laing.

Returning to creative work helped de Mille pull herself out of her doldrums. By February and March 1937, she had resumed work on new dances, and was giving recitals, sometimes dancing with Laing or to work choreographed by Tudor. His *Dark Elegies*, an emotional ballet about a village of peasants who gather to mourn the deaths of their children, introduced ballet that "incorporated steps, gestures, and body motions suggestive of modern dance; the soloists express grief, despair, and, finally, acceptance of the tragedy." (Easton, 137–138)

After another failure in a choreography job in New York (theater director Vincent Minnelli had hired de Mille to choreograph dances for the social satire production *Hooray for What!*), de Mille returned to London determined once again not to be the failure of the great de Mille family.

For years, Anna, who had been her daughter's linchpin where her career was concerned, had been encouraging de Mille to take advantage of her access to the dancers at Rambert's studio and to choreograph group pieces. With her latest failure fresh in her mind, de Mille decided to work on a project that would impress American audiences, using a large dance troupe and the collaborative efforts of Tudor and Laing. Reviving parts of other dance pieces, as well as completing a longer piece she had been working on in the summer of 1936, de Mille put together *American Suite*. It consisted of expanded versions of *The Harvesting Dust* and *'49* and included a new segment entitled *The Rodeo*.

In the summer of 1938, de Mille and the girls she trained from Rambert's school gave a London recital that included an early version of *Rodeo*. It was very well-received, but there were still a few rocky days ahead, forcing de Mille to suppress her delight. For one thing, her relationship with Tudor was beginning to show signs of strain. She performed at the Westminster Theatre in the premiere of Tudor's *Judgment of Paris*. Though de Mille considered Tudor's work brilliant, critics seemed to shower all of their accolades on de Mille's dancing. Professional jealousy festered within Tudor, and by the fall of 1938, the two were no longer colleagues or friends.

With the help of a sponsor, Tudor went off to do new work in his own theater and dance company. He didn't miss the opportunity to let de Mille know there was no place for her, because their styles were so different and, in his opinion, she was too old. In spite of her own insecurities, de Mille had never failed to tout the accomplishments of colleagues, and Tudor was no exception. She was both hurt and angry over Tudor's harsh remarks and the abrupt end of their relationship.

Perhaps everyone was being influenced by the larger threat that hung in the air over Europe—Adolf Hitler's Nazi German military had already invaded neighboring countries Austria and Czechoslovakia. A nervous Great Britain had begun preparing for the eventuality of war with Germany. The British government refused to extend de Mille's work permit, leaving her no choice but to return to America.

THE AMERICANIZATION OF BALLET

While in London, de Mille had developed her skills in story-telling and character portrayal, which she continually refined in her performances. She brought this style to the ballet world in her choreography. De Mille took lessons from Tudor, worked with him and his partner Hugh Laing, and watched and learned. Perhaps the years of working with people like Tudor and developing her own distinctive style based on training, life experiences, and individual creativity culminated in the creation of *Rodeo*.

De Mille's dance ideas always grew from an emotion, around which she would then develop a story. For inspiration, she listened to music—bold classical pieces by Bach, Mozart, and Smetana—and downed endless pots of strong tea.

AMERICAN BALLET THEATRE

When Richard Pleasant founded American Ballet Theatre (ABT), he envisioned a ballet company that would develop "a repertoire of the best ballets from the past and . . . encourage the creation of new works by gifted young choreographers, wherever they might be found." (American Ballet Theatre, "Company History") ABT made its debut at New York's Centre Theatre on January 11, 1940.

During the company's first forty years, under the creative direction of Lucia Chase and Oliver Smith, ABT offered some of the finest ballets of the nineteenth and twentieth centuries, including such classics as *Swan Lake*, *The Sleeping Beauty*, *Giselle*, *La Sylphide*, and *Rodeo*, as well as numerous contemporary pieces.

In keeping with Pleasant's vision of offering works by some of the industry's finest choreographers, ABT has commissioned choreography from the best of the twentieth century, including George Balanchine, Antony Tudor, Jerome Robbins, Twyla Tharp, and Agnes de Mille.

ABT tours the United States every year, performing for more than 600,000 people. The company has toured all fifty states and has undertaken fifteen international tours. Representatives of ABT have performed shows in 142 cities in 42 countries around the globe, including Great Britain, France, Spain, China, Japan, and Singapore.

ABT continues its commitment to acquiring the best repertoires and talents, creating new works, and bringing the enchantment of dance theater to audiences around the world.

With her environment established, de Mille developed each character's physical appearance in great detail—the appropriate type of costume, including fabric texture and color, even hair and eye color. Then she'd get up and move, creating the life of the story through movement. Sometimes it was just a gesture—the tilt of the head, the graceful wave of an arm. Other times, it was an explosion of movements—leaping across the stage as if in flight, or spiraling into a collapse on the floor to convey despair.

De Mille worked for weeks, continually developing the process. She was well versed in the arts (painting, sculpture, music, theater, and film), well educated, and familiar with cultures around the world, and she drew from these, summoning ideas based on different customs, dress, and mannerisms. One of de Mille's strengths was "her ability to find the precise gesture that conveyed a universal emotion and express it through a specific character in a specific time, rhythm, and place." (Easton, 147)

When de Mille started her career, she became one of the forerunners of a generation of choreographers who were moving away from the classical style of dance to one that was more representative of contemporary life. As a result, in the 1930s, American culture began cropping up in ballets. Choreographers around the country, including Catherine Littlefield (Philadelphia), Ruth Page, and Bentley Stone (Chicago), began incorporating "things American" into their works.

In 1935, wealthy arts patron Lincoln Kirstein established the American Ballet Company and a dance school in New York City, and hired renowned Russian choreographer George Balanchine to run both. Though the ballet company suspended operations just two weeks into its season, the school did very well. (The ballet company was resurrected fourteen years later and became known as the New York City Ballet.)

In 1936, Kirstein formed a touring group called Ballet Caravan. The dancers performed works by Balanchine and Lew Christensen. Audiences saw the infusion of jazz into the classical style of ballets. Through the works of Balanchine (*Alma Mater*), Christensen (*Filling Station*), Page and Stone (*Frankie and Johnny*), and Littlefield (*Barn Dance*), Americans first glimpsed Americana in ballet performances. In *Alma Mater*, dancers pretended to play college football; in *Barn Dance*, audiences watched square dancing.

Kirstein's Ballet Caravan performed the first successful all-American ballet in 1938, a story about a legendary Western outlaw named *Billy the Kid*. Kirstein wrote the ballet, former American Ballet student Eugene Loring choreographed the dances, and composer Aaron Copland wrote the musical score. Though *Billy the Kid* was well-received, the only ballet company that enjoyed national recognition in America was the Ballet Russe de Monte Carlo, the ballet company that had grown out of famed impresario Sergey Diaghilev's Imperial Russian Ballet.

THE BALLET RUSSE DE MONTE CARLO

Starting in 1933, the Ukrainian-American promoter Sol Hurok, who had managed Anna Pavlova's American tours, brought Colonel Wassily de Basil's Ballet Russe de Monte Carlo to New York for a season of performances. Its roster of stars included Alexandra Danilova, Tamara Toumanova, Alicia Markova, Leon Danielian, and Frederic Franklin. Americans were treated to extraordinary ballet performances.

Ballet existed in a rather small world and was often turbulent due to political and artistic competitiveness. As a result, ballet companies went through various transformations. In 1938, Russian-American Sergei Denham formed a company called the Ballet Russe de Monte Carlo, and he needed new choreographers. Denham's search was de Mille's good fortune. The slowdown in her career was about to end.

De Mille with Sol Hurok, 1952. **The American promoter and impresario Sol Hurok (1888–1974) was one of the most important figures in the development of the arts in the United States. In 1906, Hurok left a merchant's life in Ukraine for the United States; he began to arrange for musicians to entertain at meetings of the Socialist Party, and soon he had managed a booking at Carnegie Hall. At New York's Hippodrome Theatre he met dance legends Anna Pavlova and Isadora Duncan; he managed both, as well as Martha Graham and many musicians. He took charge of the Ballet Russe de Monte Carlo in 1934 and of Ballet Theatre, with Lucia Chase, in 1942. De Mille's association with Hurok began with** *Rodeo,* **which she reworked in 1942 on hearing that the Ballet Russe wanted choreography with American themes.**

"There is no definite age limit to performing once you have reached the top, but you must get there while you're young," de Mille wrote in *To a Young Dancer.* (Easton, 168) At thirty-six, de Mille realized that if she were going to have any future in ballet, it would not be as a dancer. She would have to fulfill her dream of a career in dance as a choreographer.

Joining the newly formed Ballet Theatre, founded by dancer Lucia Chase and Richard Pleasant in 1939, de Mille took on her first full-length choreography project. With a cast of sixteen untrained African-American women, de Mille created *Black Ritual*, a two-scene, twenty-five-minute piece, the first ballet ever to use African-American dancers. It was not the triumphant entry into choreography that de Mille had hoped for, but it was the first step on her path to success.

In the Ballet's second season, de Mille collaborated with dancer Sybil Shearer to revise Reed's *Three Virgins and a Devil*. Since it was a frantic, last-minute entry, de Mille danced some of the parts herself. The show was a rousing success, well received by the audience and critics. Still, it would be another three years before de Mille was commissioned to choreograph another work for Ballet Theatre.

When not working, de Mille spent time socializing with friends, including Martha Graham. One night, Graham invited de Mille to attend a concert with her and her new manager, Walter Prude. Though Prude had never heard of de Mille, he was immediately taken with her. The feeling was mutual. De Mille and Prude had much in common—they both wrote, loved music and theater, and enjoyed good literature. They dated intensely for three weeks, seeing each other almost every day before Prude was drafted and shipped off to Biloxi, Mississippi, for basic training. The two corresponded by letter often, keeping the intensity of the relationship alive. After years of disappointed romances, de Mille felt she had finally found her soulmate.

While Prude was away in Biloxi, de Mille continued to go to the dance studio to practice and do her exercises to stay in shape. Content with her personal life, she only needed a career breakthrough to make her life complete. The opportunity came one morning when de Mille bumped into an acquaintance at the studio who told her that Ballet Russe de Monte Carlo director Sergei Denham was looking for new "American-themed" dance work. De Mille immediately thought of her *Rodeo* piece. She locked herself away in her apartment, feverishly working for the next three days to revise the piece before emerging to present it to Denham. After much haggling and negotiating, Denham agreed to pay de Mille $500 for the ballet, give her complete creative control as choreographer, and let her dance the lead on opening night.

Enlisting the musical services of American composer Aaron Copland, handling costuming, set design, and rehearsals, and succeeding in the daunting task of teaching classically trained Russian dancers nontraditional ballet movements, de Mille put together a stunning smash hit for the Broadway stage. The success of *Rodeo* on opening night, October 16, 1942, confirmed her talent—after many years of disappointment, financial hardship, and failure. With the realization of her dream, de Mille would never again have to struggle for work and recognition.

In a way, *Rodeo* could have been de Mille's own story. Like the Cowgirl in the ballet, de Mille had not been very popular with boys, and had few female friends. She was often unkempt—her hair in wild disarray, her clothes shabby and unattractive—and she often felt like an outsider wishing to be accepted by her family and her profession. De Mille, unlucky in love until she met Prude, had longed for someone special with whom she could share her life. And like the lone Cowgirl, she had struggled constantly to succeed in a male-dominated business. De Mille may not have consciously paralleled her own life in *Rodeo*, but it was fitting that it should become her career breakthrough work.

8

A Life and Career Complete

1942–1954

The creative urge is the demon that will not accept anything second rate.
— Agnes de Mille

News of the smashing success of *Rodeo* spread quickly. At age thirty-seven, Agnes de Mille had realized her lifelong dream through perseverance and despite her father's disapproval, the criticism of teachers and colleagues (who had said she hadn't the right kind of body for ballet and had started to train too late), and minimal support from her family, other than that of her mother, Anna. Perhaps *No Intermissions* author Carol Easton expresses it best:

> What [Agnes] had achieved was more exciting than perfection: she had opened a window through which fresh air

Agnes de Mille in New York City, 1944. The success of *Rodeo* thrust de Mille into the spotlight of American musical theater, leading to the opportunity to work with the gifted musical team of Richard Rodgers and Oscar Hammerstein II. *Oklahoma!*, known for its seamless integration of dialogue, song, and dance, would become one of the biggest musical hits in the history of Broadway. De Mille's unique style and her capacity to bring together so many aspects of theater was fundamental to this success, and her talent set the standard for a new era in musical theater.

flooded. She had studied her craft, submitted to its discipline, and learned how, within its constraints, to be free. (194)

If the success of *Rodeo* in New York was satisfying, appearing with the Ballet Russe de Monte Carlo at the Philharmonic Auditorium in Los Angeles in the winter of 1942 was especially sweet for de Mille. With her father in attendance amid a full house, de Mille stepped onto the very stage where she had seen her beloved Anna Pavlova dance so many years ago. This time, though, it was de Mille's triumphant production, and *she* was the star.

ON TOP IN MUSICAL THEATER

Right after the success of *Rodeo*, de Mille was hired to work with the gifted composer/lyricist team of Richard Rodgers and Oscar Hammerstein on a new musical, originally entitled *Away We Go*. The show's final title would be *Oklahoma!*; it would become one of the biggest musical hits in Broadway history.

Though the American musical theater industry had some of the most talented composers around in the 1930s, including Irving Berlin, George Gershwin, and Jerome Kern, prior to the 1940s, the music was used more to match the scenery than the storyline. In 1936, George Balanchine provided Rodgers and Hart—Lorenz Hart was Rodgers's partner before Hammerstein—with a choreographed show with a touch of ballet in *On Your Toes*. But it was *Oklahoma!* that burst through the earlier theater style and altered the path of dancing in musical theater.

The storyline—a romantic triangle involving a cowboy named Curly, a pretty girl, and another man who takes her to a social—was flimsy, but de Mille would make it a signature show. Creating her own style, de Mille put together a chore-ographic ballet that was "[l]yric, non-realistic and highly stylized, but salted with detailed action that is colloquial, human, recognizable." (Easton, 201) This was a whole new way of presenting a ballet, because it was important for the audience to understand the characters through the display of emotions that could not be communicated verbally. For de Mille, acting *and* dancing were as natural as notes to a musical score.

Despite the many ego clashes throughout the production, *Oklahoma!* worked well because of the continual interplay of dialogue flowing smoothly into songs and songs into dances and back again. It was a huge hit with audiences and critics. "*Oklahoma!* was the first musical in which the libretto, score, character development, plot development, décor, stage direction, and choreography all came together; the show worked seamlessly as a whole, without sacrificing the integrity of its parts." (Easton, 207) De Mille had become one of musical theater's pioneers and innovators.

MARRIAGE AND FAMILY

De Mille married Prude in California on June 14, 1943, before he was shipped overseas. After a week's honeymoon in Los Angeles followed by three weeks spent together in New Mexico, de Mille went back to New York to start work on her next project, *One Touch of Venus.* She hired some of Martha Graham's dancers, including Sono Osato, a former Ballet Russe de Monte Carlo dancer who was of mixed Irish, Canadian, and Japanese ancestry. The collaboration among choreographer de Mille, Broadway composer Kurt Weill, dance arranger Trude Rittman, director Elia Kazan, and the dance troupe produced the musical success of the theater season. By the end of 1943, de Mille was a celebrated choreographer on Broadway.

According to dance arranger Trude Rittman, de Mille's choreography in the medium of musical theater was vastly different from that of her counterparts, including George Balanchine and Jerome Robbins. "In Agnes's work, music plays the more *dramatic* role. She begins with a *story* that develops into a dance. She conjures up emotions and pictures that music awakens in her mind. Agnes is musical; she played the piano quite well. But her foremost talent is theatrical." (Easton, 242)

De Mille with dancer in Chicago, 1943. Many new opportunities to choreograph followed the success of *Rodeo* and *Oklahoma!* De Mille began to develop her work in "modified ballet"—dance forms based on ballet technique but without the feel of classical pieces—which she hoped to popularize as a substitute for musical comedy routines. Here, de Mille works with dancers at Chicago's Civic Opera House in December 1943.

Her string of successes prompted longtime friend and theater critic John Martin to dub the new period of musicals the "de Millennium."

De Mille was in such demand that she worked almost continuously. A string of successes in the mid-1940s in both musical theater and ballet followed *One Touch of Venus*, including *Bloomer Girl, Tally-Ho,* and another Rodgers and Hammerstein collaboration, *Carousel.*

While de Mille worked stateside, success in the war in Europe had decidedly tilted in favor of the Allied forces. On May 7, 1945, the Germans officially surrendered, bringing peace to a continent ravaged by war for the past six years. De Mille at first was overjoyed to hear the news of the end of the war but then feared Prude might be transferred from England to the Pacific, where the Allies were still battling the Japanese.

During the first two years of their marriage, de Mille and Prude had not spent more than ten weeks together. Eager to see Prude in England, de Mille accepted an offer to choreograph *London Town,* a film in London, without having read the script. When she finally did read it, she was appalled. The music was terrible and the costumes outdated, and producer Wesley Ruggles was more interested in casting beautiful women than competent dancers. Likening Ruggles to her inflexible uncle Cecil, de Mille was miserable and regretted accepting the job, even if it did provide an opportunity to see Prude.

Her husband buoyed her spirits with a surprise visit, and de Mille announced before his three weeks' leave was up that they were going to have a baby. The atomic bombings of Hiroshima and Nagasaki on August 6 and 9, 1945, put an end to the war, and instead of shipping out to the Pacific, Prude headed back to New York as a civilian looking for work.

De Mille had to remain in London until November. By the time she returned to New York, Prude was working for entertainment impresario Sol Hurok. The Prudes spent the months before the birth of their baby simply adjusting to living together. Their son, Jonathan de Mille Prude, was born on April 20, 1946, with an intestinal malformation that required medical care for many years; but becoming a mother made de Mille finally feel complete. "What I got from childbirth was the sense of belonging to a race, being part of a big organic natural thing." (Easton, 251)

De Mille secured the nanny services of Lily Cantelo, who had been her maid in London, and hired Lily's husband, Charles, as her chauffeur and handyman. She began getting back in shape and resumed teaching her "Acting for Dancers" classes. Since the success of *Oklahoma!*, de Mille was much in demand as an instructor.

INCREASING WORK IN MUSICALS

Despite the war, pregnancy, and motherhood, the 1940s were a prolific time in de Mille's career. Besides working with Rodgers and Hammerstein on three musicals (their third was the less successful *Allegro* in 1947), de Mille was also tapped to work with the musical duo Alan Lerner and Frederick Loewe. Her first project was *Brigadoon*, a transatlantic romance set in Scotland and New York. (She would choreograph *Paint Your Wagon* for Lerner and Loewe in 1951.)

Though de Mille once again had to assert that the choreography was as important as the other elements of the show (music, lyrics, and acting), *Brigadoon* ultimately received unanimous praise from critics. In fact, *Life* magazine said, "*Brigadoon*'s real brilliance lies in its Scottish dances directed by Agnes de Mille." (Easton, 261) The choreography for *Brigadoon* was so well-received that it netted de Mille her only Antoinette Perry Award ("Tony"), which she won in a tie with Michael Kidd for *Finian's Rainbow*.

The success of *Brigadoon* was bittersweet for de Mille, because her mother, Anna, died just a few days after the show made its Broadway debut on March 13, 1947. De Mille could find consolation in knowing that her mother had lived to see her succeed in her career and in her personal life, and to see her grandson, Jonathan, born. Anna had never accepted her divorce from William or his remarriage, and de Mille often felt guilty about her devotion to her father, despite the hurt he had inflicted on Anna. Still, whenever reminiscing about her mother, de Mille always gave Anna her due, acknowledging the sacrifices she had made in order to help her daughter succeed.

De Mille's choice of Prude as a partner turned out to be very wise. She needed a dominant man in her life, just as her father had been. Prude was stubborn, extremely independent, and as strong-willed as de Mille. He was also enjoying his own success managing the careers of concert stars such as violinist Isaac Stern, guitarist Andrés Segovia, and opera divas Marian Anderson and Roberta Peters. To maintain career independence, it was important for Prude and de Mille to move and socialize in separate circles, with their own professional colleagues. When they entertained guests, though, they did so together, with de Mille deriving great pleasure in planning the details. They were content with their life together and with their careers.

The next big theatrical success for de Mille was an adaptation of the story of the New England schoolteacher Lizzie Borden, who was accused of murdering her parents with an axe in 1892. Fascinated by the gruesome ever since childhood, when she had witnessed a snake consuming a frog at Merriewold, de Mille choreographed what many consider her ballet masterpiece—*Fall River Legend*. Lucia Chase of Ballet Theatre contracted de Mille to choreograph *Fall River Legend* for the 1948 season as a kind of apology for the company's mishandling of two of her other ballets, *Tally-Ho* and *Three Virgins and a Devil*, in the company's European debut in 1946.

De Mille had always felt ill-treated by the company, which had Chase as its financier, Oliver Smith as codirector, and Antony Tudor as its artistic director and the only choreographer on staff. Though de Mille probably would not have been suited for the position of artistic director, it had always bothered her that she had never been offered a job on the company's staff. For various reasons, her relationship with

RODGERS AND HAMMERSTEIN

The composer Richard Rodgers and the lyricist Oscar Hammerstein II, both born in New York City, became two of the most influential and successful artists in the film and theater industries. The musicals they created in their seventeen-year collaboration earned thirty-four Antoinette Perry ("Tony") Awards, fifteen Academy Awards, two Pulitzer Prizes, two Grammy Awards, and two Emmy Awards.

Rodgers, who was born in 1902, began his composing career in the 1920s when he partnered exclusively with Lorenz Hart to produce a series of musicals for Broadway, London, and Hollywood. Between 1920 and 1940, Rodgers and Hart collaborated on such Broadway and Hollywood hit musicals as *A Connecticut Yankee*, *The Phantom President*, *I Married an Angel*, and *Pal Joey*. Hart's untimely death in 1942, at the age of 48, brought an end to their success.

Oscar Hammerstein II, born in 1895, came from a family deeply involved in the arts: His grandfather had been a famous opera impresario, his father managed a theater, and his uncle was a successful Broadway producer. While studying law at Columbia University, Hammerstein wrote lyrics for the college's varsity shows. Hammerstein actually worked with Rodgers and Hart while at Columbia, cowriting the lyrics to *Fly With Me*

Ballet Theatre continually eroded, but she was pleased to have the opportunity to work on *Fall River Legend.*

Despite being unable to work with the dancers until about three weeks before the New York opening, de Mille produced a ballet that *New York Times* theater critic John Martin heralded as "the revelation of a woman's soul" and "beautifully consistent, an ingenious and intuitive melodrama that not

with Hart. In 1923, Hammerstein's first commercial success, *Wildflower*, established him as a creator of beautiful lyrics for the operetta art form. He worked with some of the great composers of the time, including Sigmund Romberg and George Gershwin.

While Hammerstein was redefining the voice of operetta, Rodgers and Hart were breaking barriers in musical theater. The prolific partnership of Rodgers and Hammerstein began a year after Hart's death. Their first project was *Oklahoma!*, which blended musical comedy and operetta to create a whole new style in theater—the musical play. During the next sixteen years, Rodgers and Hammerstein created some of the most memorable songs and shows in Broadway history, including *Carousel, South Pacific, The King and I*, and *The Sound of Music.*

Oscar Hammerstein's death in 1960 ended one of the greatest collaborations in musical and theatrical history. In 1990, Richard Rodgers was honored by Broadway when the 46th Street Theatre was renamed the Richard Rodgers Theatre. The greatest tribute to Hammerstein's work came in 1995, when revivals of his musicals *Showboat, The King and I*, and *State Fair* all appeared on Broadway simultaneously.

only makes the pulses beat rapidly but draws tears more than once." (Easton, 284)

ANOTHER CAREER EMERGES

Because of de Mille's terrific sense of drama and visual effect, her talents were best suited to the theatrical genre of opera. She would have the opportunity to direct only one, though— *The Rape of Lucretia*. The cast enjoyed working on the project, but it played to mixed reviews with audiences and critics, closing after only twenty-three performances.

De Mille continued to take dance classes, and she choreographed other Broadway shows, including *Gentlemen Prefer Blondes*. The show included the Jule Styne song "Diamonds Are a Girl's Best Friend," which became the signature song of its wide-eyed, young, platinum-blond star, Carol Channing.

While working on *Gentlemen Prefer Blondes*, de Mille met her match in stubbornness and volatility with Styne. Though he admired her talent, Styne said of de Mille, "[she] never thinks about how good the show is. She thinks about how good Agnes de Mille is. She was a Take Charge. She mixed in on direction, she mixed in on a lotta areas. . . . Not meaning to hurt, but just flaunting her know-how." (Easton, 294) Styne echoed the sentiments of many others who worked with de Mille—she was well respected, but many of her colleagues didn't *like* her.

After a disastrous experience as director on Cole Porter's *Out of This World*, de Mille channeled her energies into nurturing a writing career. While pregnant with Jonathan, de Mille had begun to write her memoirs in composition books, on hotel stationery, and on any bits of paper available. Eventually, the manuscript found its way to the publishers Little, Brown and Company. What was later entitled *Dance to the Piper* was de Mille's account of the first thirty-seven years of her life—as a de Mille, as a struggling dancer, and, finally, as a successful choreographer and wife. Within

Fall River Legend. De Mille was fascinated by the horror of the notorious Lizzie Borden case, in which a Massachusetts woman was accused of the gruesome murders of her father and step-mother. In 1948, acknowledging that it had mishandled two of her earlier works, Ballet Theatre offered de Mille a commission to choreograph a piece about Borden—*Fall River Legend.* Although de Mille had only three weeks to work with the dancers, the show was a great success, and *Fall River Legend* is now considered de Mille's masterpiece. This photograph is from a 1953 performance; at the far left is Lucia Chase, one of the founders of Ballet Theatre.

weeks of its publication in January of 1952, *Dance to the Piper* became a best-seller.

At the pinnacle of her profession in ballet and theater, as a successful author, an adored wife, and a mother, de Mille had snatched the brass ring; but she had worked very hard to reach the heights she had dreamed of for so long. She'd find staying on top almost impossible.

Though de Mille would work on several more Broadway shows, Lerner and Loewe's *Paint Your Wagon* was really the last of the type of Broadway musical that bore her trademark style. A group of younger artistic men and women were rising through the ranks of the dance world—Jerome Robbins, Hanya Holm, Anna Sokolow, Michael Kidd—who benefited from the path already forged by de Mille. Jobs were going to others—de Mille's difficult temperament caused colleagues to pass on her services when shows such as *Brigadoon* and *Paint Your Wagon* were brought to the big screen. A fight with Alan Lerner cost her the chance to choreograph the next Lerner and Loewe collaboration—*My Fair Lady*, one of the biggest musical hits in theater history.

In 1953, de Mille again stretched her creative wings and formed her own company, the Agnes de Mille Dance Theatre. In a four-month period, the company traveled more than 36,000 miles, performing in cities across the country and even in Canada. After the company's fall opening in Baltimore, Maryland, de Mille returned to New York to work on another forgettable show, *The Girl in Pink Tights*.

By the 1950s, de Mille had been creating dances for more than two decades. Her most distinguished colleagues, George Balanchine and Martha Graham, had carved their own places in dance history, with very different results. Balanchine's ballets "dazzled." Graham's dances were "mythic." De Mille's works were "human."

After watching a performance of *Paint Your Wagon*, de Mille realized that her choreography had a sameness about it.

According to biographer Carol Easton, "The recurring theme in [Agnes's] choreography (and in *Dance to the Piper*) was prefigured in her childhood: paradise lost and the futile attempt to regain it. Her preoccupations were nature, love, sex, and death." (Easton, 335) In even the most serious stories, de Mille almost always managed to break the emotional tension with a joke. She once explained to critic Walter Terry that she probably did that because she never really had any faith in the development of emotion.

9

Expanding Her Craft

1954–1993

I want one word on my tombstone—*dancer*.

—Agnes de Mille, 1993

Another foray into the world of motion pictures was as unsatisfying to de Mille as *Cleopatra* had been in 1934. Hired in 1954 by Rodgers and Hammerstein to choreograph the dances for the film version of *Oklahoma!*, de Mille again tried to plan the dances in a way that dominated the film instead of being secondary to the story. It did not matter that she worked grueling hours or that she considered the dances to be her finest work. Because of additional costs and the time required to pare down or excise the dances, de Mille had infuriated and alienated two more colleagues.

In her mind, de Mille felt rejected again by Hollywood, and she left unfulfilled. Shortly after returning to New York, she had

124

Agnes de Mille in 1956. Late in her career, de Mille began to share her perspective on life, art, and dance through books and educational lectures. Lending her voice of influence as an advocate for the rights of professionals in her field, she organized the Society of Stage Directors and Choreographers (SSDC). She would become president of the SSDC in 1965—the first woman to serve in the role of president of a national labor union.

to weather another emotional blow. Her father, William, having been ill with cancer for some time, died in the spring of 1955. With his death, de Mille was left with many unresolved issues in her relationship with William, issues that had almost always been recurring themes in her dances.

Work was always the panacea for de Mille, and in 1956, she even returned to the stage, dancing the role of the Cowgirl during a European tour of Ballet Theatre (now known as

American Ballet Theatre). Despite being fifty years old, she pushed herself relentlessly into shape and danced as if she were twenty years younger. The reviews were stellar, giving de Mille an affirmation of her talents. Though it wasn't intended to be a farewell performance, it was a wonderful way to wind up her tenure in the Europe she had left eighteen years earlier.

De Mille's career had been evolving and broadening for some time. She seemed to be in step with the changing world in the 1950s. She was already working on her next book, *And Promenade Home* (published in 1957), and she was building a nice lecture career. At the invitation of Sarah Lawrence College president Harold Taylor in 1951, de Mille spoke at the dedication of the school's new art center. Not long after, she became a member of the college's distinguished board and gave lectures at other educational institutions about the arts and dance.

A new medium of entertainment—television—allowed yet another expansion of her career, one that gave de Mille the opportunity to bring her lectures into living rooms across the country. *Omnibus*, an educational series funded by the Ford Foundation, featured programs on music appreciation, history, and law, to name a few. In 1952 and 1953, *Omnibus* had televised de Mille's ballets *Rodeo* and *Three Virgins and a Devil*, two of the first complete ballets ever broadcast on television. For the 1956 season, de Mille prepared and narrated two programs: "The Art of Ballet" (aired February 26), and "The Art of Choreography" (December 30).

Never before had one person in dance ever reached so many people from so many walks of life. The reviews and accolades poured in. Said Joseph Welch of *Dance Magazine*, "Millions of people awoke the morning of February 26, 1956, possessing either no knowledge of the ballet or at best a dim perception of this ancient, beautiful art. That night those same millions fell asleep with their lives enriched and their hearts gladdened. . . . They had looked at *Omnibus* and seen Miss de Mille's 'The Art of Ballet.' " (Easton, 356)

For her last appearance on *Omnibus* in 1957, de Mille prepared a full program about the Lizzie Borden case, discussing the crime, staging a reenactment of the murder and ensuing trial, and ending the show with a full-length performance of *Fall River Legend*. De Mille had found a new medium not only to educate people about dance, but to produce dance performances. As Walter Terry wrote, "Miss de Mille has done a wonderful job . . . in bringing the excitement and the dignity and the urgency of dance to television." (Easton, 357)

A LIFE LESS FRENETIC

Life for de Mille, now in her late fifties, seemed to have less urgency. She no longer felt a burning need to prove herself, with her worth in her profession no longer in question. She spent much of her time writing, giving her lectures, and being a wife and mother. She had time to travel or to relax at Merriewold.

In 1958, she returned to Broadway to choreograph two shows—*Goldilocks*, a labor of love for which she was nominated for a Tony Award, and *Juno*, which was just a labor.

In 1959, an appearance on Edward R. Murrow's television show *Small World* electrified de Mille's lecture career. Going toe-to-toe with gossip columnist Hedda Hopper about politics in the arts, de Mille showed her ability to improvise and brilliantly express her opinions, backed by substantiated facts. Suddenly standing-room-only audiences were filling auditoriums to hear de Mille talk. She expanded her lecture repertoire on the arts to educate on the importance of having orchestras, operas, ballets, and other musical art forms and the necessity for private and public funding. Said de Mille, "There has never been great art without great patronage." (Easton, 373)

At the beginning of the 1960s, de Mille was working on two books: *To a Young Dancer*, something of a guidebook for potential students on teachers, recitals, auditions, and other aspects of the industry, and *The Book of Dance*, a tome on the cultural history of dance. The latter was, in the words of *Dance Observer*, "the crowning laurel in Agnes de Mille's highly distinguished literary career." (Easton, 377)

A CHAMPION OF THE ARTS AND CHOREOGRAPHERS

For a long time, it had been de Mille's dream to found a national folk theater, or "heritage theater," where singing, dancing, and acting could flourish. Something of that magnitude required substantial funding, and de Mille had grave difficulty acquiring such funds. When the Ford Foundation turned down her request for a $100,000 grant, de Mille recognized her new goal—to fight for government support for the arts.

In 1961, de Mille returned to Broadway. Working with *Brigadoon* director Robert Lewis, she choreographed all seventeen dances for *Kwamina*, an interracial love story set in Africa. Praised by critics for its brave attempt to treat a difficult subject and for its dances, the show nevertheless closed after only a month's run. For *Kwamina*, de Mille received the third Tony nomination of her illustrious career (she had won for *Brigadoon* in 1947).

Becoming more involved in causes, de Mille was a vocal advocate of the rights of choreographers to engage in collective bargaining. Up until 1962, choreographers and stage directors had no union, no bargaining power, no copyright protection, and no secondary rights to their works, such as movie and television rights. Only composers, playwrights, lyricists, dancers, and actors had such protection. De Mille was one of those who, having no union representation, lost a lot of money that would have otherwise been due her. Her oratory skills and her outrage over those injustices made de Mille the logical voice for the cause. With the assistance of Shepard Traube, who was organizing a union for theatrical directors, de Mille was able to get choreographers incorporated into the group that became known as the Society of Stage Directors and Choreographers (SSDC). She would become the SSDC's president in 1965, becoming the first woman president of a national labor union.

After a few more shows, de Mille devoted most of her time to her lectures and her continued efforts to get funding for a "heritage" folk theater. President John F. Kennedy and his wife, Jacqueline, were huge supporters of the arts and were interested in helping to preserve them. Though Kennedy didn't live to see it, the National Council on the Arts and Humanities was established in 1965. De Mille was among those included, along with John Steinbeck, Leonard Bernstein, David Brinkley, and Gregory Peck, on the first advisory panel. With a $5 million endowment, the panel intended to provide grants for the enrichment and expansion of the arts.

In the mid-1960s, de Mille began receiving awards of recognition for her accomplishments in her field. In 1966, New York Senator Jacob Javits presented de Mille with the Capezio Dance Award, calling her "a generative catalyst of determination, courage, and vision who had enriched, enlivened and enlarged the horizons of the American dance and the American Theatre." (Easton, 410)

Work was less frequently offered by this time, and de Mille and Prude seemed content to enjoy their free time together. Son Jonathan graduated from Amherst College in 1970, going on to Harvard with a fellowship in history.

In 1973, the Prudes celebrated their twenty-fifth wedding anniversary at a party thrown by longtime friend Oliver Smith. Now in her late sixties, de Mille was still active, writing and lecturing, and overseeing a new dance company she formed with students in North Carolina with the help of grants. It was difficult to keep the company afloat financially, but the touring experiences were invaluable for the young students.

After the touring season ended, de Mille reworked her lecture presentations, incorporating into her talks film clips, tapes, and music to enhance her discussion of dance in its many

Working with dancers on *Gold Rush*. As the popularity of television increased, de Mille found a new avenue of expression. Several televised programs featured her choreography, and her involvement in the educational series *Omnibus*, which was funded by the Ford Foundation, made the high-art world of dance and theater accessible to more people than ever before. Here de Mille, looking on from the background, works with dancers during a rehearsal for *Gold Rush* (1965), a televised version of de Mille's *'49*.

contexts in society—political, historical, and cultural. She tried the new format out over the summer at some speaking engagements and received a terrific response. In the fall of 1974, de Mille presented the production in several cities in combination with her heritage program. The complete production became known as *Conversations About the Dance*, the culmination of de Mille's talents as an entertainer and writer.

LIFE AS A DANCER ENDS

In 1975, de Mille received an appreciation from the North Carolina School of the Arts. To raise more funds for her heritage program, de Mille planned a special showing of *Conversations About the Dance* on May 15, 1975, for representatives of some of the foundations, who might decide to contribute. Just hours before the showing, a blood vessel in de Mille's brain burst, causing a massive cerebral hemorrhage that paralyzed the right side of her body and severely impaired her vision, speech, memory, and mobility.

De Mille's condition was critical for weeks, and she remained hospitalized for more than three months. Blood clots in her right leg and her carotid artery required her to undergo two surgeries in her already weakened condition. When she finally was able to go home, she had regained her sight and ability to speak, but her right side remained paralyzed. With physical therapy, de Mille regained some semblance of function, but the unencumbered life she had lived until her seventieth year was clearly over.

Losing control of part of her body functions devastated de Mille. The body that once moved fluidly at her command became a prison. It took months to relearn phone numbers, to hold a pen and write, to move her right arm an inch, to walk. Never again could she glide across a room or dance floor— now walking with a leg brace and cane without stumbling was a triumph. De Mille saw herself as clumsy and unattractive. Once vibrant and full of energy and ideas, de Mille now felt old.

She would not be defeated, though. Even if she could no longer dance, she was determined to be creative, to communicate, and to contribute. In the hospital, de Mille began using a tape recorder to work on her next book, *Where the Wings Grow*, a memoir of her time at Merriewold. Continuing to fight, de Mille made a recovery beyond anyone's expectations, except perhaps her own. Cards and letters from friends and admirers lifted her spirits and spurred her on. By 1976, de Mille was walking much better with the brace. With the help of an assistant, she returned to the lecture circuit.

On July 8, 1976, at a gala in her honor, de Mille made her first public appearance since her stroke. Standing behind a lectern, she told the audience, "[H]ere I stand before you, although I thought never to stand again." (Easton, 443) Oliver Smith read a letter from President Gerald Ford, and de Mille was presented with the Handel Medallion, New York City's highest award for artistic achievement. The audience was then treated to performances from *Rodeo*, *Fall River Legend*, and *Texas Fourth*. It was the most memorable night of de Mille's career.

On a stop in Easton, Maryland, de Mille visited her sister, Margaret, who was losing her battle with cancer (she died in 1978). Though she tried to be encouraging, de Mille felt powerless to help Margaret.

As Prude's own health began to deteriorate, de Mille was being thrust into the spotlight by colleagues and admirers for her gritty determination to live her life to the fullest despite her physical limitations. She was showered with awards, received standing ovations wherever she appeared, and was viewed as a national treasure rather than a dance icon.

THE PHOENIX RISES

De Mille remained busy, writing her second book after her stroke, *Reprieve*, about life after a stroke. In October 1977, de Mille finished the work she had started on *Conversations*

About the Dance on the day of her stroke. From a chair, she triumphantly conducted the two-hour show. Enough grant money was acquired to take *Conversations About the Dance* into the studio to be recorded and broadcast on public television in 1980. De Mille was also working on a biography of Martha Graham, which would be published after Graham's death in 1991, and another book titled *America Dances.*

In 1979, de Mille saw her name back in lights on Broadway with the revival production of *Oklahoma!* In 1980, the *grande dame* of dance received the Kennedy Center Career Achievement Award. In 1983, she was the guest of honor at "A Memorable Evening of Dance Honoring Agnes de Mille," a kindly roast of de Mille by esteemed friends and colleagues. In 1986, de Mille was presented the National Medal of the Arts by President Ronald Reagan during a White House luncheon.

Son Jonathan had married and gave de Mille two grandsons, David, born in 1982, and Michael, born in 1987. Prude continued to struggle with cervical arthritis and had trouble getting around. He and de Mille, with their physical impairments, often had accidental falls, which they treated with amusement. Still, Prude was able to raise his glass to toast his wife at her eightieth birthday party.

De Mille continued to work as best she could, mostly at home in bed. Determined to put together a ballet using many of the dances from the failed *Juno*, de Mille wrote *The Informer.* It premiered on March 15, 1988, though ill health prevented de Mille and Prude from attending.

By summer, Prude's health was failing. On August 29, the unimaginable moment in de Mille's life came—her beloved Walter passed away. In a private burial at Merriewold under rainy skies, de Mille said farewell: "Walter darling, we've been married for forty-five years, and in all that time I was never bored." (Easton, 459)

Life without Prude was quieter, lonelier. De Mille kept busy, working on Graham's biography and occasionally dining

A tribute to Agnes de Mille. De Mille's efforts to support the preservation of the arts contributed to the establishment of the National Council on the Arts and Humanities (1965). De Mille served on the first advisory panel of the organization, allocating an endowment of $5 million for grants for the development of the arts. Many awards recognized her accomplishments, and she remained a powerful presence in her profession until the time of her death. New York's Shubert Theater hosted a tribute to de Mille in May of 1983; with her were dancers Natalia Makarova and Mikhail Baryshnikov.

out or attending a movie with friends. She began work on what would be her final ballet, *The Other*, another remembrance of her childhood days at Merriewold. *The Other*, an American Ballet Theatre production, premiered at the Kennedy Center for the Performing Arts on April 3, 1992.

In the spring of her eighty-eighth year, de Mille accepted a special Tony Award commemorating the fiftieth anniversary of *Oklahoma!* In June, American Ballet Theatre (ABT) put on what was to be its final tribute to de Mille, presenting *The Informer*, *Three Virgins and a Devil*, and *Rodeo*. After the second intermission, the curtain rose to reveal de Mille seated on the stage alone. Trying to quell a standing ovation, de Mille implored the audience to support ABT, which was in serious financial trouble. It was a fitting final appearance—de Mille was still fighting for the arts to which she had devoted her life.

The summer passed with de Mille still striving to learn and keep active. She rarely thought of her own mortality, preferring to focus on whatever work she could handle. On October 6, 1993, after a busy day, de Mille enjoyed a belated birthday dinner with her friend Paul Moore before retiring. Sometime during the night, she suffered another stroke, this one fatal. Thus ended the life of one of the most prolific, tireless people in the history of dance and the arts.

In *No Intermissions*, Carol Easton writes of de Mille:

> Described as "perhaps the best dancer ever to write and the best writer ever to dance" de Mille communicated her thoughts in words, her feelings in dance, and her wonderful sense of the ridiculous in both. But her greatest achievements were neither her choreography nor her writing, nor her ability to speak eloquently, in places of power, for all dancers; it was the totality of her spirit.

1905 Born Agnes George de Mille on September 18 in New York City to Anna George and William de Mille.

1914 De Mille family moves to Hollywood, California.

1918 Begins taking ballet lessons at the Theodore Kosloff School of Imperial Russian Ballet.

1926 Graduates cum laude from the University of California, Los Angeles; the next day, Anna and William announce their intention to divorce.

1927 Begins performing professionally, introducing dance pieces *Stage Fright*, *Ballet Class, '49*, and others.

1929 Hired for her first professional choreography job, *The Black Crook*; begins dance partnership with Leonard Warren.

1932 Suffers her first flop with *Flying Colors*; leaves for London, where she meets Marie Rambert, Antony Tudor, and Hugh Laing; makes the acquaintance of Ramon Reed.

1933 Choreographs *Nymph Errant* in London.

1934 Hired by her uncle Cecil B. de Mille to choreograph dances for his movie epic *Cleopatra*.

1935 Choreographs dances for George Cukor's film *Romeo and Juliet*.

1936 Choreographs Leslie Howard's *Hamlet* in New York; Ramon Reed dies.

1939 American Ballet Theatre is founded by Lucia Chase and Richard Pleasant.

1942 Finally achieves her career breakthrough with *Rodeo*.

1943–1944 Marries Walter Prude on June 14, 1943; has a string of hits, including Rodgers and Hammerstein's *Oklahoma!*, *One Touch of Venus*, *Tally-Ho*, and *Bloomer Girls*.

1945 Reunites with Rodgers and Hammerstein to create *Carousel*.

1946 Choreographs *London Town*; son, Jonathan de Mille Prude, is born on April 20.

1947 Now dubbed the "Queen of Broadway," de Mille collaborates with Lerner and Loewe on *Brigadoon*; mother, Anna, dies on March 15; de Mille again teams up with Rodgers and Hammerstein on *Allegro*; wins an Antoinette Perry (Tony) Award for *Brigadoon*.

1948 Creates *Fall River Legend*, based on the story of Lizzie Borden; the ballet is presented by American Ballet Theatre.

1951 Again teams with Lerner and Loewe on the Broadway production of *Paint Your Wagon*.

1952 Publishes her first autobiography, *Dance to the Piper* (she would go on to write several other books, including a biography of Martha Graham); moves away from Broadway musical work and produces the major ballet *The Harvest According*.

1953 Forms the Agnes de Mille Dance Theatre and takes the company on a 126-city tour.

1954 Makes a return to motion pictures, choreographing the film version of *Oklahoma!*, which does not go well; she is not hired to work on *Carousel* the following year.

1955 William de Mille dies of cancer.

1959 Earns a Tony nomination for *Goldilocks*; appears as a guest on Edward R. Murrow's *Small World* television show and speaks out on freedom of speech; her appearance receives a rave response, galvanizing de Mille's lecturing career on topics such as funding and support for the arts.

1962 Premieres *The Wind in the Mountains* with American Ballet Theatre; earns a Tony nomination for *Kwamina*.

1965 Elected president of the Society of Stage Directors and Choreographers, becoming the first woman president of a national labor union.

1966 Receives the Capezio Dance Award.

1972 Forms the Heritage Dance Theatre with students from North Carolina.

1975 Suffers a massive cerebral hemorrhage, leaving her right side paralyzed; she remains hospitalized for three months.

1976 In her first public appearance after the stroke, she is awarded the Handel Medallion, New York's highest award for artistic achievement.

1977 Conducts *Conversations About the Dance* seated in a chair; the show is later filmed for public television and broadcast in 1980.

1978 Sister, Margaret, dies of cancer.

1980 Receives the Kennedy Center Career Achievement Award.

1986 Receives the National Medal of the Arts.

1988   Husband, Walter Prude, dies on August 29 at age 79.

1993   Receives a special Antoinette Perry (Tony) Award
       commemorating the fiftieth anniversary of *Oklahoma!*;
       at age 88, suffers a fatal stroke on the evening of
       October 6.

Works by Agnes de Mille

Theatrical Choreography

Stage Fright, 1927

Ballet Class, 1927

'49, 1927

The Black Crook, 1929

Flying Colors, 1932

Nymph Errant, 1933

Oklahoma!, 1943

One Touch of Venus, 1943

Bloomer Girl, 1944

Carousel, 1945

Brigadoon, 1947

Allegro, 1947

Gentlemen Prefer Blondes, 1949

Paint Your Wagon, 1951

The Girl in Pink Tights, 1954

Goldilocks, 1958

Juno, 1959

Kwamina, 1961

110 in the Shade, 1963

Come Summer, 1970

Ballets

Obeah, Black Ritual, 1940

Three Virgins and a Devil, 1941

Drums Sound in Hackensack, 1941

Rodeo, 1942

Tally-Ho, 1944

Fall River Legend, 1948

The Harvest According, 1952

The Rib of Eve, 1956

Sebastian, 1957

The Bitter Weird, 1962

The Rehearsal, 1964

The Wind in the Mountains, 1965
The Four Marys, 1965
Golden Age, 1967
A Rose for Miss Emily, 1970
Texas Fourth, 1973
Summer, 1975
A Bridegroom Called Death, 1978
Inconsequentials, 1981
The Informer, 1988
The Other, 1992

Books

Dance to the Piper, 1952
And Promenade Home, 1958
To a Young Dancer, 1962
The Book of Dance, 1963
Lizzie Borden: A Dance of Death, 1968
Speak to Me, Dance with Me, 1973
Where the Wings Grow, 1978
America Dances, 1980
Reprieve: A Memoir, 1981
Portrait Gallery, 1990
Martha: The Life and Work of Martha Graham, 1991

Other

The Ragamuffin, 1916 (appearance in a film written and
    directed by William de Mille)
Cleopatra, 1934 (film)
Romeo and Juliet, 1935 (film)
London Town, 1946 (film)
Conversations About the Dance, 1980 (television)

Bibliography

De Mille, Agnes. *American Dances: A Personal Chronicle in Words and Pictures.* Obolensky/Macmillan, 1980.

———. *Dance to the Piper.* Atlantic-Little, Brown, 1952.

———. *Speak to Me, Dance with Me.* Atlantic-Little, Brown, 1973.

Easton, Carol. *No Intermissions: The Life and Times of Agnes de Mille.* Little, Brown and Company, 1996.

Ford, Carin T. *Legends of American Dance and Choreography.* Enslow Publishers, 2000.

Gherman, Beverly. *Agnes de Mille: Dancing off the Earth.* Athenum/Macmillan, 1990.

Golden, Kristen. *Remarkable Women of the Twentieth Century.* Friedman/Fairfax Publishing, 1998.

Long, Robert Emmett. *Broadway, the Golden Years: Jerome Robbins and the Great Choreographer-Directors, 1940 to the Present.* New York: Continuum International Publishing Group, 2001.

Books

Block, Geoffrey, and Fred L. Block. *Enchanted Evenings: The Broadway Musical from* Show Boat *to Sondheim.* Oxford University Press, 1997.

Freedman, Russell. *Martha Graham: A Dancer's Life.* Clarion Books, 1998.

Garafola, Lynn. *Diaghilev's Ballets Russes.* Da Capo Press, 1998.

Kaye, Elizabeth. *American Ballet Theatre: A 25-Year Retrospective.* Andrews McMeel Publishing, 1999.

Kislan, Richard. *The Musical: A Look at the American Musical Theater.* Applause Books (revised edition), 1995.

Web Sites

American Ballet Theatre
www.abt.org

Gaynor Minden/Dancer.com: Great Ballerinas: Anna Pavlova
www.dancer.com/Pavlova.html

The John F. Kennedy Center for the Performing Arts/
Kennedy Center Honorees
**www.kennedy-center.org/programs/specialevents/honors/
history/honoree/demille.html**

The Official Martha Graham Web Site
www.marthagrahamdance.org

The Rodgers and Hammerstein Organization
www.rnh.com/index1.html

Index

Index

Index

page:

13: Courtesy Library of Congress, LC-USZ62-126396
20: © Bettmann/CORBIS
23: © Bettmann/CORBIS
27: © Bettmann/CORBIS
37: © Bettmann/CORBIS
41: © Hulton/Archive by Getty Images
49: © Hulton/Archive by Getty Images
53: © Bettmann/CORBIS
62: © John Springer Collection/CORBIS
65: © Hulton-Deutsch Collection/CORBIS
73: © E.O. Hoppé/CORBIS
76: © Bettmann/CORBIS

79: © Hulton/Archive by Getty Images
83: © Hulton/Archive by Getty Images
92: © Bettmann/CORBIS
95: © Bettmann/CORBIS
101: © Bettmann/CORBIS
107: © Bettmann/CORBIS
111: Associated Press, AP
114: © Bettmann/CORBIS
121: © Hulton-Deutsch Collection/ CORBIS
125: Associated Press, AP
130: © Hulton/Archive by Getty Images
134: © Bettmann/CORBIS

Cover: © Bettmann/CORBIS

Contributors

Judy L. Hasday, a native of Pennsylvania, received her B.A. in communications and her Ed.M. in instructional technologies from Temple University. Ms. Hasday has written many books for young adults, including New York Public Library "Books for the Teen Age" award winners *James Earl Jones* (1999) and *The Holocaust* (2003), and *Extraordinary Women Athletes,* a National Social Studies Council "2001 Notable Social Studies Trade Book for Young People."

Congresswoman Betty McCollum (Minnesota, Fourth District) is the second woman from Minnesota ever to have been elected to Congress. Since the start of her first term of office in 2000, she has worked diligently to protect the environment and to expand access to health care, and she has been an especially strong supporter of education and women's health care. She holds several prominent positions in the House Democratic Caucus and enjoys the rare distinction of serving on three House Committees at once. In 2001, she was appointed to represent the House Democrats on the National Council on the Arts, the advisory board of the National Endowment for the Arts.